Pre-Kindergarten/ Kindergarten Teacher Guide Year Blue, Semester 1

By Debbie Trafton O'Neal (Core) and Anne M. Dunham (Bonus)

This teacher guide accompanies the Pre-Kindergarten/Kindergarten Learner Resource and the Age 2–Grade 4 Teacher Class Kit.

Bible Backgrounds: Janet M. Corpus
Editors: Pamela Foster and Eileen K. Zahn
Designer: Carl Nelson, Chance•Nelson, Inc.
Illustrators: Leann E. Johnson, Pamela Johnson, and Stacey Schuett

JOOS

ISBN 0-8066-4756-6

Augsburg Fortress
www.augsburgfortress.org

Sunday School Curriculum

Contents

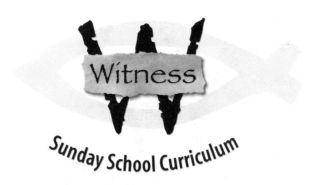

Introduction

Welcome to Witness!

Witness Sunday School Curriculum is a great way to teach the kids you know and care about how to "Learn from the Bible to Live the Good News." What is the good news? God promises, provides, and is present throughout human history. God the Father, Son, and Spirit is for us and with us, wherever we are and whatever we do. God is also for others: in our homes, in our neighborhoods, in our churches, and all around the world. That is news worth sharing!

As God's children—young and old, teachers and learners—we are witnesses to God's action in the world. Our salvation story is a story of God's gifts of Word, faith, and service. Each of these gifts functions as both meaningful connection and joyful invitation. Word connects us with the biblical story and invites us to use our minds to learn, make good choices, and communicate with others. Faith connects us with God's family and invites us to explore and affirm our identity as the church. Service connects us with our sisters and brothers, using Jesus as our model, and invites us to act lovingly for them. In Witness, your learners will encounter many ways to witness to others by exploring how they can express their faith in daily life with family, friends, the broader community, and God's creation.

Sunday school teachers play a valuable role in the faith development of young children. Whether you're a teaching veteran or a first-time teacher, this teacher guide will provide what you need to plan and carry out lively, engaging, and meaningful Sunday school sessions for your learners. Witness is designed to support teachers as they prepare for teaching children! Keep reading to learn more about Witness Sunday School Curriculum.

How Should I Get to Know Witness?

First, read pages 2-5 carefully. Then leaf through the Core and Bonus sessions in this teacher guide. Take a look at the leaflets and stickers in the learner resource. Explore the posters, activity cards, and reproducible sheets in the teacher class kit. Listen to the audio CD in the teacher class kit. Get familiar with the abbreviations for the learner resource (LR), teacher guide (TG), and teacher class kit (TCK).

What's in the Teacher Guide?

The teacher guide (TG) contains everything you need to know to teach up to 20 Sunday school sessions this semester. In addition to these introductory pages, this teacher guide contains age-level information on page 5, step-by-step plans for teaching 15 Core sessions on pages 6-80, an introduction to Bonus sessions on page 81, step-by-step plans for teaching five Bonus sessions on pages 82-91, and reproducible learner pages for Bonus sessions on pages 92-96. The inside front cover lists the scope and sequence for this semester. A family letter is found on the inside back cover. Make copies of this letter to distribute to learners during the first Sunday school session of the semester.

What's in the Learner Resource?

The learner resource (LR) contains two pages of color stickers and 15 four-page color leaflets to be used during the 15 Core sessions. To reduce week-to-week preparation time, prepare all of the leaflets and stickers before the semester begins. Separate the nested leaflets and group them by session. Cut apart the stickers and store them by session in small, resealable bags. Use folders or an accordion file to keep the materials for each session separate. Since many session activities require you to show pictures and read directions from the leaflet, make sure you have your own leaflet each week.

What's in the Teacher Class Kit?

Witness teacher class kits (TCK) are terrific for both learners and teachers. They contain posters, activity cards, reproducible sheets, and an audio CD. Many TCK items were designed for use in specific sessions, but some items support teaching and learning throughout the

Learn from the

course. Hang the colorful posters in your class area. Some have a biblical theme and some are designed to help learners connect the Bible to life. Use the activity cards and reproducible sheets to tell stories and creatively reinforce Bible learning. Copy reproducible sheets for each learner to use during storytelling, art activities, and games. Among the reproducible sheets in each kit are those used as learner resources for Bonus sessions. Play a track from the audio CD each week and enjoy the varied formats and clever approaches to the Bible stories that use both music and spoken word.

What Are Core Sessions and Bonus Sessions?

There are two types of Witness Sunday school sessions: Core and Bonus. Each semester, the teacher guide contains 15 Core sessions that follow the salvation story. During the first semester of each Witness year, most Core sessions are based on stories from the Old Testament. A few sessions at the end of Semester 1 focus on New Testament stories. These stories help learners prepare for Advent and Christmas. During the second semester of each Witness year, all Core sessions have New Testament stories as their basis, most from the Gospels of Luke and Matthew.

Each teacher guide also contains five Bonus sessions for each semester. These sessions offer added variety and flexibility. Read more about the Bonus session format on page 81.

What Is the Format of Each Core Session?

Each Core session is five pages long and describes everything you need for a 60-minute Sunday school session. The first page contains a session-at-a-glance chart that lists estimated activity times, needed materials, and learner activities. Find the Bible Text, the Key Verse, and the kid-friendly Big Idea statement on this page to prepare for presenting the story.

On the second page you'll find the Bible Background, Learner Goals, and Age-Level Connection to enrich your preparation. Look for the Teacher Prayer and Question for Reflection in the sidebar for additional support and encouragement. Learner Goals carry out the Witness theme and broaden both teachers' and learners' understanding of the story. These goals match the characteristics of a witness: someone who knows the Word, grows in faith, and shows service. These Learner Goals also carry through to home, because the back page of each leaflet provides ways for families to know, grow, and show. The

third, fourth, and fifth pages of each session describe what happens during your time with learners. Two factoids in each session provide additional background about the Bible story. Information about the material you will need and any preparation you should do before class appear as M&P before each activity. Note that activity times on each page are suggestions; expand or shorten depending on your learners' interests, classroom characteristics, availability of materials, and other factors.

Ready for the Story provides ideas for greeting learners and giving them something to do as others arrive, introduces a part of the story through one or more of the senses, and involves all learners in movement. Sidebar items include Witness Words and Transition Tip. Post the Witness Words, teach them during class, include them in word games and puzzles, or use them in other creative ways. Transition Tips help you shift to Explore the Story and may involve movement, signals, or props.

Learners hear the Bible story during Explore the Story. Use the Bible art and storytelling script on the second page of the leaflet for Storytelling. After setting up and telling the story, follow the teacher guide's suggestions for discussing the Faith Trait. Sidebar items include Kid Connect and More Movement. Kid Connect helps you engage kids in conversations and activities that are connected to the story. Use the movement activity when learners would enjoy moving their bodies.

Live the Story helps learners apply the story to their own lives and offers ideas for sharing the story and witnessing to others. Creative activity options like Kids Create mean kids can take home original art to help remember the story. Sidebar items on this page include Witnesses in the World, Teacher Boost, and Great Goodbyes. Go Global! is a sidebar in Sessions 1, 4, 7, 9, and 13. Before Session 1 copy Reproducible Sheets I and J (TCK), back to back, for each child. Plan how to use the puzzle with each session that has a Go Global! activity.

Note: Most sidebar items (More Movement, Transition Tip, Witnesses in the World, Go Global!, and Great Goodbyes) contain activity suggestions. Because these activities are optional, materials and preparation are not found in the session-at-a-glance chart. Read ahead and plan accordingly!

What Is FAITH Traits?

Faith Traits is an exciting part of Witness that teaches faith-based character and values to kids. Each session relates one Faith Trait to a Bible character and provides one or more activities that develop the trait in learners during the Sunday school session and at home. With the inspiration of Bible characters, the guidance of the Spirit, and the support of others in their faith community, Faith Traits strengthen kids to be disciples.

Witness teaches 24 Faith Traits that stem from God's Graces of love, trust, courage, and hope. Love manifests itself as the Faith Traits of generosity, kindness, humility, compassion, empathy, respect, and thankfulness. Trust appears as the Faith Traits of cooperation, loyalty, obedience, boldness, and reverence. Courage shows itself as the Faith Traits of responsibility, self-discipline, perseverance, forgiveness, justice, honesty, and wisdom. Hope shines forth as the Faith Traits of harmony, stewardship, patience, peace, and joy.

Several items in the teacher class kit will help you teach Faith Traits and each session leaflet will include the Faith Trait as well.

How Should I Get Ready for Sunday School?

Find out all you can about your learners—especially what children that age enjoy and how they like to learn. Plan how you will *prepare yourself* to teach each week. Focus on what God's good news means for your life and your learners' lives.

Stock your classroom with basic supplies like paper, markers or crayons, scissors, glue sticks, and tape. Use adhesive putty, tape, or pushpins to display posters from the teacher class kit. Some posters are designed for use during specific sessions; others can be displayed for the entire semester. Make copies of the reproducible pages (TG) and sheets (TCK) as you need them so that you have the correct number. The more you do ahead of time, the more time you will have to chat with kids as they arrive.

What Kind of Space Do I Need to Teach Witness?

Witness sessions can be used in a traditional classroom space with a table and chairs. Many activities encourage the use of comfortable spaces for storytelling and open spaces for movement. Pillows, beanbags, and other soft seating arrangements encourage learners to relax and enjoy stories. Carpet squares give each child a defined space when sitting in rows or a circle. Before playing games that involve lots of movement, remove obstacles to make sure your learning space is safe.

How Can I Connect with My Learners?

Develop a warm relationship with each learner to build a positive foundation for learning and teaching in your Sunday school group. Connecting with your learners will help them feel important and valued in the group and loved by God.

■ Welcome each child by name each week and use names often. Sit or kneel so you are at eye level when you talk. Ask questions about activities, pets, family members, and other people and things important to kids.

■ Encourage peer relationships! Use name tags and play name games to help learners remember their peers' names. Plan cooperative activities so everyone works toward one goal. Pay attention to how learners connect with each other in pairs, small groups, and all-boy or all-girl groups, and use the groupings that work.

■ Become familiar with all learners' special needs, including allergies. Sensitivities to peanuts and latex can be life-threatening.

■ Provide alternative ways to participate when activities ask for hugging, since some kids are uncomfortable with this type of touching. Handshakes, high fives, and pats on the shoulder may be preferred.

■ Ask learners to help with group tasks such as passing out leaflets, pressing the CD player button to start a song, and collecting art materials. Offer enthusiastic and genuine thanks for their help.

■ Create consistency in Sunday school sessions so learners know when activities begin and end. You might use a chime or bell to signal a change to the next activity, or flip the lights on and off.

■ Pray for your learners and the teaching ministry in your congregation.

Age-Level Characteristics

Nurturing faith in Sunday school involves building relationships and understanding kids. Age is one of the biggest factors in determining how kids will learn and act. Here are some general characteristics of Pre-Kindergarten/Kindergarten learners, some ideas for building relationships in your classroom, and a few tips for sharing God's good news in kid-friendly ways.

Learn from the Bible to Li

Pre-Kindergarten and Kindergarten kids:

- Are full of energy.
- Think concretely and literally.
- Show developing large-muscle and small-muscle skills.
- Believe in fairness as a measure of right and wrong.
- Enjoy playing cooperative games.
- Revel in music and dance.
- Are curious and creative.
- Are proud of their accomplishments.
- May be learning to read.
- May be able to write their names and a few letters.
- Are intrigued by new information.
- Prefer to sit on the floor rather than in chairs.
- Need to experience love.
- Are beginning to play with others, in addition to playing side by side.
- Like to share stories about themselves, their families, and their friends.
- Enjoy being a part of a group.
- Are active, but can sit for short periods.
- Think by asking questions.
- Are sensitive to criticism, their feelings easily hurt.
- Learn by doing.
- Enjoy hearing stories read aloud.
- Vary in their physical development and interests.

To nurture faith and build relationships with these kids:

- Learn their names.
- Celebrate birthdays and baptismal anniversaries.
- Ask them about their lives each week.
- Listen actively and carefully.
- Provide a safe place for them to share their stories.
- Have fun together.
- Celebrate their accomplishments.
- Provide a predictable classroom routine, and enlist their help, such as passing out materials, cleaning up, and turning out the lights.

- Let them know you are their friend.
- Share parts of your own faith journey.

To facilitate friendships between kids:

- Play name games.
- Plan activities to help kids get to know each other.
- Play cooperative team games.
- Provide opportunities to work together in pairs and small groups.

To help them learn from the Bible to live the good news:

- Show them where the stories come from in the Bible.
- Invite them to become characters in the story and dramatize it.
- Hide story props around the room and invite them to search for them, then use them to tell the story.
- Explore many aspects of a Bible story with a variety of activities that use different types of skills and abilities, such as cooking, going outside, playing games, doing a treasure hunt, and solving puzzles.
- Provide opportunities for them to share Bible stories with other children.
- Witness in the world by planning service projects to help families with kids, such as collecting clothing, toys, and kid-friendly food.
- Lead learners in prayers for children in your community and throughout the world.
- Use rhythm, music, and dance to actively involve the kids in a musical rendition of the story.

A Final Word

As a Sunday school teacher, you share the Word, express your faith, and serve God and others. At Augsburg Fortress, everyone involved in the writing and production of Witness sincerely hopes that these materials meet your teaching needs and help you and your learners travel further on your faith journeys. Contact us at witness@augsburg fortress.org with your Witness stories! God bless you and your learners!

the Good News

God Creates People

Bible Text

Genesis 2:4b-25

Key Verse

I praise you, for I am fearfully and wonderfully made. Psalm 139:14

God trusts us with all creation.

LR = Learner Resource
TCK = Teacher Class Kit
M&P = Materials and Preparation

Session at a Glance	What You Need	What Learners Do
Ready for the Story (15 minutes)		
Welcome the Witnesses	• Witness CD (TCK), Posters E and G (TCK), CD player, poster board, crayons or markers, paper punch, yarn, scissors	• Make name tags.
Story Warm-Up	• Plastic place mats, playdough, people and animal cookie cutters	• Make playdough animals and people.
Story Fire-Up	• Small hand mirror, box with lid, masking tape	• See someone who is special to God.
Explore the Story (20 minutes)		
Story Set-Up	• Leaflet 1 (LR), Poster K (TCK), Activity Card D (TCK), scissors, crayons or markers, removable tape, flowers or plant	• Color God's beautiful world.
Storytelling	• Poster C (TCK), Witness CD (TCK), Leaflet 1 (LR), CD player	• Hear the Bible story of when God created people.
Faith Traits	• Sticker Sheet 1 (LR), Poster K (TCK), poster board, magnetic tape, scissors	• Learn about the Faith Trait of generosity.
Live the Story (25 minutes)		
Ways to Witness	• Posters C and D (TCK), Leaflet 1 (LR), crayons or markers	• Discover ways to take care of God's world.
Kids Create	• Construction paper, marker, paintbrushes, washable paint, paint shirts, hand wipes or water and paper towels • 5" x 7" (13 cm x 18 cm) picture frame mats, markers, decorative items, glue, mirror	• Make handprints on a class poster. • Decorate picture frame mats.
Wrapping It Up	• Leaflet 1 (LR), Bible	• Review the Bible story and Key Verse.

Bible Background — What Factors Shaped This Story?

Genesis 1 tells the "days" of creation story. Genesis 2 focuses on the creation of human beings and their role in caring for the rest of creation (see 2:15). We call the first human Adam after the Hebrew word *adam* for the creature that God forms from the *adamah* or ground. The first human is a "ground creature," an "earth creature." Human beings are inextricably bound to the earth from which we were formed. God created a partner for Adam from Adam's own rib. The close connection between man and woman is established by God and forms the basis of the partnership of marriage (2:24).

What Is This Story About?

God creates the earth and the heavens. Without rain or anyone to tend the land, there is no vegetation. God forms a human being and breathes life into it. God creates a garden—not "wild" plants—where God puts the human being to till and keep the garden. The human was free to eat except from one tree. God created animals and birds as partners for the human, who named the other creatures. No partner was adequate as a helper until the creation of woman. Verses 10-14 describe geography, vouching for the historical nature of God's action.

Why Is This Story Important?

The creation stories tell what is important to know about God and ourselves. God is the creator of all that is in earth and the heavens. God creates human beings from creation (the ground), making them—us—inseparable from creation. Divine breath enlivens human beings, making us dependent on God. God created human beings to care for creation's vegetation. To be human as God created us is to be partners with all the other creatures, especially other human beings.

Age-Level Connection

Preschoolers and kindergartners are eager to be together and learn new things. If this is one of their first experiences in a classroom, some may be hesitant or shy to join group activities. Make a special point to welcome each child by name and with a smile.

Teacher Prayer

Thank you, Lord, for this new day, and for all days when I can appreciate, enjoy, and wonder at the world you have created! Help me to lean on you as I meet with these children and begin a journey with them, a journey to learn more about you. Amen

Question for Reflection

How can you show the children they are special to you and to God?

Learner Goals

KNOW

God made all people special

GROW

in understanding that God loves all people

SHOW

love and care to others

FACTOID

We have many names for God. *Lord* translates YHWH (sometimes pronounced "yah-way"), the Hebrew name for *God* in Genesis 3:14.

WORDS

Adam, Eve, garden

FACTOID

The Tigris and Euphrates Rivers flow from what was Mesopotamia through Babylonia into the Persian Gulf. The Pishon and Havilah rivers are unknown today.

▶ **Transition Tip** ◀

Make sure the playdough is out of sight during storytelling to avoid distractions. Have the children sit with their legs crossed in front of them as you gather to read the Bible story.

Ready for the Story *(15 minutes)*

Welcome the Witnesses

M&P *Display Posters E and G from the Age 2–Grade 4 Teacher Class Kit (TCK) where they can stay up for all sessions. Locate the Witness CD (TCK) and a CD player. Cut 6" (15 cm) circles from poster board, punch a hole at the top of each one, and tie a 20" (51 cm) length of yarn through it to make a name tag for each child.*

Play the CD as the learners arrive. Print the learner's name on a name tag as each arrives. Help learners put on their name tags to help you learn their names more quickly. **Welcome to our Sunday school class! I'm so excited we'll be learning about God's love together!**

Story Warm-Up

M&P *Make or purchase playdough, and have available people and animal cookie cutters and plastic place mats. To make playdough: Combine 2 cups (480 ml) flour, 1 cup (240 ml) salt, and 4 teaspoons (20 ml) cream of tartar in a saucepan. Stir in 2 cups (480 ml) cold water mixed with 4 table-spoons (60 ml) oil and several drops of food coloring. Cook over medium heat, stirring constantly until a ball forms. Store in a covered container.*

Invite the learners to sit at a table where you have put place mats, playdough, and the cookie cutters. As the learners roll and form the playdough into shapes, talk about the Big Idea for this session. **God trusts us with all creation. What does the word *creation* mean?** Talk about the playdough creations they are making, and ask what other things they like to make or create. **God is the best creator of all. God made the world and all that is in it! God even made people to enjoy the beautiful world.** Ask learners to put the playdough back in the container.

Story Fire-Up

M&P *Fasten a mirror inside a box with a lid, such as a shoe box.*

I have something very special inside, something that God created! Would you take a peek inside and see what it is? Using the box you have prepared, go from learner to learner, letting each child peek into the box. **What did you see? Were you surprised? God made each of us special and unique. We are created by God to live in the beautiful world!**

8

Explore the Story (20 minutes)

Story Set-Up

M&P *Gather Leaflet 1 from the Pre-Kindergarten/Kindergarten Learner Resource (LR). Cut apart the sentence strips on Activity Card D (TCK) and follow the directions on the card for storage. Have the Session 1 Big Idea sentence strip available and display Poster K (TCK) (laminate, if possible) where everyone can see it. Have available removable tape and crayons or markers, and bring a bouquet of flowers or a potted plant to brighten up the classroom.*

Ask one of the learners to distribute the leaflets and crayons or markers. Read the title aloud. Point out the color code, inviting learners to color the scene by matching the shapes with colors. Ask questions as learners work. **Do any of you have gardens at home? Do you like to work in the garden? What kinds of things do you like to plant?** As the learners finish their pictures, point out the Big Idea on the back of their leaflets and read it aloud. Ask for a volunteer to tape the Big Idea sentence strip to the space on Poster K. **What does it mean to trust someone?** *(Accept learner responses.)* **You trust your family and friends because you know they love you and won't hurt you. Why do you think God trusts us with all creation?**

Storytelling

M&P *Display Poster C (TCK) where everyone can see it. Have Track 1 ready on the Witness CD (TCK). Make sure each learner has Leaflet 1 (LR).*

Point out the poster and discuss the creation scene pictured. Invite the learners to think about some of the beautiful things they have seen in creation. **Isn't it awesome that God made so many different things for us to enjoy in the world? It would be boring if everything and everyone in the world were exactly the same!** Play Track 1 of the CD and learn the song about creation together. Have the learners turn to the inside of their leaflet and look at the illustration of creation. **In the Bible story for today, we will talk about one of the most creative things God did. God made people!** Read the Bible story aloud to the learners as it is written, then ask if they noticed anything that repeated in the story. Reread the story, encouraging the learners to join you in saying, **And God made you and me! Point to someone else, then to yourself, as you say it.** Read the Key Verse aloud.

FAITH Traits

M&P *You will need the Session 1 Faith Trait sticker on Sticker Sheet 1 (LR). Gather a sheet of poster board for each child, magnetic tape (available from office or craft supply stores), and scissors to complete the Faith Traits puzzle.*

There are so many things we can learn together as children of God! We can learn how to be generous to others. To be generous or have generosity means to share freely with others. How has God been generous to us? Show the learners the Faith Trait sticker for Session 1. Help each learner write his or her name on a sheet of poster board. (Save the poster board for use in each session.) Have the learners attach the Faith Trait sticker to the poster board and cut around the shape of the sticker. Attach a piece of magnet tape to the back. **Each week you will make a new piece of a Faith Traits puzzle to take home. Soon you will have all of the pieces to make the puzzle.**

Kid Connect

One of the important ways we can care for God's creation is by recycling. Show the learners examples of the kinds of materials that can be recycled: paper, glass, and aluminum. Explain that besides recycling things to make new materials, recycling can also mean giving something that is still good to someone else to use, or making something new from it.

More Movement

For learners who are not used to sitting in a classroom, a break for movement would be great. Play a simple recycling game. Give each learner something that can be recycled, such as paper, plastic bottles or cups, or an aluminum can. Put a line of tape down the center of the area. Then use cues such as, "Whoever has something plastic to recycle, stand on this side of the line." Everyone who has a plastic item will stand on one side of the line and everyone who does not will stand on the other side of the line. Play this game for several minutes, being sure to name all of the items the learners have.

Teacher Boost

You made it! This first session can be challenging as you try to accomplish many things: getting to know the children, sharing information about God's love, and keeping the pace realistic for young children. Think about what went well this session and what you might do differently next time you meet.

Witnesses in the World

How can we treat others as the special children of God that they are? Share ideas about the kind things we can do for others at home, at school, on a sports team, or in our neighborhood. Encourage learners to think about being extra kind to others this week.

Go Global!

Check out the Session 1 Go Global! activity on Reproducible Sheets I and J (TCK). See page 3 of this guide.

GREAT good byes

Play Track 1 of the Witness CD (TCK). Encourage learners to think of motions to the song as they wait for their parents and caregivers to pick them up. Make it a point to greet each family and tell each child that you are so glad he or she was here and that you look forward to seeing him or her next week. Keep the name tags for use in Session 2.

Live the Story (25 minutes)

Ways to Witness

M&P *Display Poster C (TCK). Each learner needs Leaflet 1 (LR) and crayons or markers.*

God created such a beautiful world! But sometimes people don't take care of it. Turn Poster C over to display Poster D. **What is different about this picture? How can people take better care of God's world? What would need to happen in this picture? How do you take care of God's world?** Most young children have definite ideas about environmental issues, whether it involves picking up trash, throwing trash away in a trash can rather than littering, or recycling materials they use. Now have the learners turn to the third page in the leaflet and draw two ways they can care for God's world.

Kids Create (Choose One!)

M&P *"God Made Me Special" Poster: Before class, print "God Made Me Special" at the top of a large piece of construction paper. Have available different colors of washable paint, paintbrushes, paint shirts, and hand wipes (or a small tub of soapy water and paper towels).*

Mirror Picture: You will need one 5" x 7" (13 cm x 18 cm) picture frame mat for each learner, plus markers, glue, and decorative items such as foam pieces and stickers, and a mirror as big as the mat.

"God Made Me Special" Poster: Have each child put on a paint shirt. Use a paintbrush to paint one of each child's hands, then spread her or his fingers apart and press the painted side down on the paper to make a handprint. Print each child's name next to their handprint. Have learners wash their hands in the tub of water and dry them off with paper towels. Set the poster aside to dry, then hang it in the classroom. **God made each of us special and unique. Our handprints and fingerprints are different from anyone else's in the entire world!**

Mirror Picture: Put the decorative items on the table and give each learner a picture frame mat. Encourage them to decorate their frames as creatively as they choose. Hold a frame against a mirror. **Look! Inside this frame is someone who is very special to God!** Encourage the learners to take their frames home and attach them to a mirror where they can look every day to see someone who is special to God.

Wrapping It Up

M&P *Have a Bible and one Leaflet 1 (LR) available.*

Ask the learners to gather their leaflets and any projects to take home and set them aside. Gather together in a circle on the floor. Open your Bible and read the Key Verse, Psalm 139:14, aloud. **I praise you, for I am fearfully and wonderfully made.** Have the learners repeat this verse aloud with you. **God made each person in the world special! You are one of God's special children too!** Show the back of the leaflet and explain that there are things on this page to share with their families and do together at home. Then ask the learners to fold their hands with you as you pray. **Dear God, thank you for making all of us special! Amen**

Jacob and Esau

Session at a Glance	What You Need	What Learners Do
Ready for the Story (15 minutes)		
Welcome the Witnesses	• Witness CD (TCK), CD player, name tags from Session 1, materials for making name tags	• Listen to the CD and find their name tags.
Story Warm-Up	• Play home center, toy cooking utensils, aprons, chef's hats	• Pretend to cook and serve food.
Story Fire-Up	• Posters L and H (TCK)	• Learn about different kinds of families.
Explore the Story (20 minutes)		
Story Set-Up	• Leaflet 2 (LR), Sticker Sheet 2 (LR), Activity Card D (TCK), Poster K (TCK)	• Learn about two brothers.
Storytelling	• Leaflet 2 (LR), Activity Card C (TCK), white paper, scissors, crayons, removable tape, plastic straws or craft sticks	• Hear the story of Jacob and Esau and make story puppets.
Faith Traits	• Sticker Sheet 1 (LR), magnetic tape, poster board, scissors	• Learn about the Faith Trait of loyalty.
Live the Story (25 minutes)		
Ways to Witness	• Leaflet 2 (LR), Activity Card B (TCK)	• Match pairs of twins.
Kids Create	• Felt, felt or foam pieces, glue, permanent marker • Three colors of thick yarn or cord, scissors, masking tape, beads	• Make blessing banners. • Make friendship bracelets.
Wrapping It Up	• Bible	• Review the Faith Trait and Key Verse.

Bible Text

Genesis 27:1-40

Key Verse

But Esau ran to meet [Jacob], and embraced him. Genesis 33:4

God claims each of us.

LR = Learner Resource
TCK = Teacher Class Kit
M&P = Materials and Preparation

Teacher Prayer

Lord, thank for you my family and friends! Sometimes I get so wrapped up in what I'm doing that I neglect them or take them for granted. Help me to keep a good perspective and balance with taking care of those I love. Amen

Question for Reflection

How can I balance my time more evenly between work, family, and leisure activities?

Learner Goals

KNOW

God wants us to love others

GROW

in understanding how to show others we care

SHOW

loyalty to friends

FACTOID

Blessing and curse are opposites frequently contrasted in the Bible. Both express relationship. Blessing speaks favor on someone. Cursing speaks evil.

Bible Background | What Factors Shaped This Story?

Rebekah, like some other women in the Bible, was blessed with children though she had been thought barren and past childbearing age. Isaac prayed to God and Rebekah and Isaac's twins were conceived. Genesis 25:19-34 tells of the twins' struggle with one another even before they were born. As children, Esau, who was the older, was favored by their father, Isaac; Jacob was favored by their mother, Rebekah. It was normal for the oldest son to be the prime inheritor. However, in the Bible we read stories of second sons usurping the first son's position.

What Is This Story About?

This is a story of treachery and deception within a family. Out of favoritism, Rebekah set herself and Jacob against Esau. In doing this, she also betrayed Isaac. Why couldn't Isaac distinguish his sons? His questions reveal his suspicions, but Isaac was blind. Isaac could not tell by sound which son was greeting him. As twins, they may have had very similar voices. Although Isaac recognized Jacob's voice, Rebekah betrayed Isaac's senses of smell and touch, dressing Jacob in Esau's clothes. She used animal skins to disguise Jacob's smooth hands for Esau's hairy ones. Isaac's remaining sense—taste—was the one with which, in eating Jacob's savory food, the betrayal was made complete. It was also over a meal that earlier (25:29-34) Esau sold his birthright to Jacob.

Why Is This Story Important?

The patriarchs of Jewish and Christian traditions are Abraham, Isaac, and Jacob, related as father, son, and grandson. (Today we also acknowledge their partners Sarah, Rebekah, Leah, and Rachel, the latter two Jacob's spouses.) This story tells a crucial turn of events that affected how that important lineage came to us. Personal, community, political, and even international relationships intertwine. What happened in this family affected the history of the ancient people of God. It was from Jacob's descendants, whose name became Israel, that God formed a chosen people. We also see that God chooses and uses imperfect people like us from imperfect families such as our own.

Age-Level Connection

Some young children have brothers and sisters or close relatives with whom they spend a lot of time. Others are the only children in their families. Only children sometimes have a harder time sharing, taking turns, and noticing how their words or actions might affect others than children with siblings do. Watch for class opportunities to offer gentle reminders of these times and model them yourself to help children learn how to treat others in kind and thoughtful ways.

Ready for the Story (15 minutes)

Welcome the Witnesses

M&P *Locate the Witness CD from the Age 2–Grade 4 Teacher Class Kit (TCK) and a CD player. Put out the name tags from Session 1 (page 8) where the learners can find theirs and wear them. Have name tag materials available for new learners this week.*

Play the CD as the learners arrive. Sing along with the Track 1 song that you learned in Session 1 and encourage the learners to sing along. Greet parents and caregivers as they drop their children off. Encourage everyone to put on her or his name tag and review names.

Story Warm-Up

M&P *You will need access to a home center or play area with cooking utensils, aprons, chef's hats, and so on. Or bring these items from home and allow learners to play with them in your space.*

Invite the learners into the home center area you have prepared and encourage them to pretend to cook, mix, and bake. If possible, have a small table and chairs where they can set the table and pretend to serve food to others. If you include a phone in the area, you may be surprised by how many children will use the phone to order pizza! As the children are pretending and playing, talk to individuals about some of their favorite foods to eat. **What is your favorite food?**

Story Fire-Up

M&P *Display Poster L (TCK) where everyone can see it. Have Poster H (TCK) ready.*

Look at all of these different families! We are all part of families too. Invite the children to share things about their families. You may want to guide them with the things they include, such as how many people are in their family, if they have a pet, and maybe something special their family likes to eat together. Be sensitive to the fact that families are different: some children may live with a single parent, others may come from a divorced family, have stepparents, or live with grandparents. Share things about your family too. **Besides the families we live with at home, we are all part of another family—God's family! The people in God's family are part of this church, but people in God's family also live all over the world! Some of the people in God's family lived a long time ago.** Now show learners Poster H. Point out different Bible families to the learners; some of the learners may recognize certain Bible families but not all of them. **Isn't it amazing that we are all part of God's family?**

Witness WORDS

loyal, friendship, honesty

FACTOID

Jacob and Esau are the progenitors of the Israelites and the Edomites between whom there is conflict (2 Samuel 8:12-14; 2 Kings 8:20-22).

► **Transition Tip** ◄

To help learners make a transition from one activity to another, consider choosing a signal they will recognize, such as ringing a bell, shaking a tambourine, or flicking the lights on and off. Be sure to explain this signal to the children before using it so they won't be startled.

Kid Connect

Are there twins in your class or congregation that the children might know? Talk about different kinds of twins: some twins are identical while others are not. And even though twins may look the same, they won't necessarily think or act the same.

More Movement

Play Track 2 of the Witness CD (TCK) and listen to it together. **What actions would fit this song?** Encourage the learners to think of different actions, then act out the song using them.

Explore the Story (20 minutes)

Story Set-Up

M&P *Gather Leaflet 2 from the Pre-Kindergarten/Kindergarten Learner Resource (LR) and the Jacob and Esau sticker from Sticker Sheet 2 (LR). Display Poster K (TCK) and have the Session 2 Big Idea sentence strip from Activity Card D (TCK) and removable tape available. Remove the Session 1 sentence strip from the poster and display the strip somewhere in the classroom.*

Ask for a volunteer to distribute the leaflets. Read the title aloud. Read about Jacob and his brother Esau, and invite the learners to complete the picture by adding the sticker of the two brothers to the rock. Review the Session 1 Big Idea sentence strip that you have removed from Poster K and displayed in the classroom. Point out the Big Idea printed on the back of the leaflet, and read it aloud to the learners. Choose a learner to tape the Session 2 Big Idea sentence strip to the space on the poster. **When God claims us, it means that God wants us and loves us. How do you know that you are special to God and a child of God?** *(Encourage ideas.)* **Remember that no matter what, you will always be special to God.**

Storytelling

M&P *Gather Leaflet 2 (LR), plastic straws or craft sticks, scissors, and tape. Trace an outline of each story figure from Activity Card C (TCK) on white paper. Copy the sheet of outlines for each learner. Prepare the story figures from Activity Card C (TCK) by cutting out and attaching the figures to straws or craft sticks with removable tape.*

Ask the learners to turn to the inside of their leaflets, and look at the Bible story picture together. Use the puppet figures you made to help retell the story. Read the story from the leaflet, moving the puppet figures for emphasis. Afterward, give each learner a copy of the puppet figure outlines to color, cut out, and attach to straws or craft sticks. Provide help as needed. **Sometimes brothers and sisters have fights or say mean things to each other. They can be mad, but still love each other. One of the good things that happened to Jacob and Esau is that when they were older they forgave each other. Our Bible verse is from that time: "But Esau ran to meet [Jacob], and embraced him." When you embrace someone, you hug them. Isn't it good that people can forgive each other?**

FAITH Traits

M&P *You will need the Session 2 Faith Trait sticker on Sticker Sheet 1 (LR), magnetic tape, each learner's poster board, and scissors.*

Today the Faith Trait is loyalty. Being loyal means to always be friends with someone, to stick with him or her no matter what. How can you be a loyal friend? *(Accept all answers.)* Discuss ways of showing loyalty, including ways suggested by the children. Have the learners attach the Faith Trait sticker to the poster board next to the space where they cut out the last piece. Help them cut the poster board around the shape of the sticker and attach a piece of magnetic tape to the back. Encourage learners to add this piece to their puzzle at home.

Live the Story (25 minutes)

Ways to Witness

M&P *Have available Leaflet 2 (LR). Prepare Activity Card B (TCK) for a matching game.*

Invite the learners to turn to the next page in their leaflets, and talk about the things good friends do for each other. **What are some ways that friends help each other?** Ask learners to share their own experiences, then help them identify and match the situations on the page. Gather together at a table or on the floor and put the cards face down. One child starts by turning over two cards. If the cards don't match, the child turns the cards facedown and the next child turns over two cards. If the two cards match, the child keeps the matching cards. Then the next learner takes a turn, and so on until all the matches are found. Repeat this game until everyone has had a turn to turn over cards. **What do notice about the twins on the cards? Do they look the same? Do you know any twins?**

Kids Create (Choose One!)

M&P *Blessing Banners: Locate a 9" x 12" (23 cm x 30 cm) sheet of felt for each child, assorted felt or foam pieces, glue, and a permanent marker.*

Friendship Bracelets: Cut 12" (30 cm) lengths of three different colors of thick yarn or cord for each learner. Have beads and masking tape available.

Blessing Banners: Give each learner a felt sheet for a banner. **What does it mean to be blessed?** Invite learners to share some of the things they are blessed with, such as a loving family, pets, and good friends. Have them arrange and glue felt or foam pieces to their felt banners to remind them of some of their blessings. Be sure to add each learner's name with a permanent marker. **Have someone help you hang this in your room to remind you of how blessed you are!**

Friendship Bracelets: Tie one length of each color together at one end. Demonstrate how to braid the three pieces together. Tape the knotted end of each set to a table for easier braiding. Children's abilities vary widely, so be prepared to offer extensive help. (If learners have trouble braiding, provide beads for them to string onto the yarn as an alternative.) When the children have finished, tie off the end of the bracelet in a single knot, making sure it fits around each learner's wrist securely but not too tightly. **These bracelets can remind you that God is always with you.**

Wrapping It Up

M&P *Have a Bible available.*

Gather in a circle on the floor. Open your Bible and read the Key Verse, Genesis 33:4, aloud. **Even when we disagree with someone, it is good to forgive and love that person! A loyal friend would do that.** Remind the learners about the back of the leaflet and mention some of the fun things they can do with their families that are printed on that page. Ask the learners to fold their hands and bow their heads to pray with you. **Thank you, Lord, for good friends, brothers and sisters, and for choosing us as your special children! Amen**

Teacher Boost

Make your room child-friendly. Kneel and look around the area before or during the session today. Kneeling, you're about at the learners' level. What do you see? What is difficult to see? Display posters or other learning tools at the children's eye level, rather than at yours.

Witnesses in the World

Does your congregation sponsor or support a care facility such as a nursing home or child-care center? Such facilities can often use supplies, and when budgets are tight donations are appreciated. Check with someone in your congregation who might know about these organizations. Your class could decorate a box to collect donations. Put a sign on it to explain what donations are requested and where the donations will go, send a note home with learners, and put a notice about what your class is doing in the church bulletin, newsletter, and Web site.

GREAT good byes

Bend down to the children's eye level and say a special good-bye to each child. Remind them that they are claimed and chosen by God and you are glad they are part of this class.

Joseph's Dreams

Bible Text

Genesis 37:1-11

Key Verse

Once Joseph had a dream.
Genesis 37:5

God knows we can do great things.

Session at a Glance	What You Need	What Learners Do
Ready for the Story (15 minutes)		
Welcome the Witnesses	• Witness CD (TCK), name tags, CD player	• Listen to a CD and find name tags.
Story Warm-Up	• Play farm animals, toy farm equipment and people, toy barn, building blocks	• Play with a farm set.
Story Fire-Up	• Poster O (TCK)	• Talk about dreams and how God speaks to us today.
Explore the Story (20 minutes)		
Story Set-Up	• Leaflet 3 (LR), Sticker Sheet 2 (LR), Posters K and Q (TCK), Activity Card D (TCK), removable tape	• Learn about what shepherds do.
Storytelling	• Leaflet 3 (LR), simple props and costumes	• Learn and act out the story of Joseph and his brothers.
Faith Traits	• Sticker Sheet 1 (LR), magnetic tape, poster board, scissors	• Learn about the Faith Trait of wisdom.
Live the Story (25 minutes)		
Ways to Witness	• Leaflet 3 (LR), crayons or markers	• Learn about making good decisions.
Kids Create	• Large paper bags, crayons or markers, scissors • Embroidery hoops, tape, colorful ribbon	• Make colorful coats. • Make hoop streamers.
Wrapping It Up	• Poster T (TCK)	• Review the Bible story and Big Idea.

LR = Learner Resource
TCK = Teacher Class Kit
M&P = Materials and Preparation

Bible Background — What Factors Shaped This Story?

Jacob (later renamed Israel) had two spouses (Leah and Rachel), two concubines (Leah and Rachel's maids, Zilpah and Bilhah, respectively), and 12 sons. Jacob also had daughters (37:35). Jacob favored Rachel and Joseph, her firstborn son. At the time of this story, Rachel was deceased. Reuben, Jacob's firstborn, was first of Leah's six sons, and Judah was the fourth. Abraham and Sarah, Isaac and Rebekah, and Jacob and his spouses and their families had been nomads. By God's leading (35:1) Jacob settled with his family in Bethel. Jacob's 12 sons were progenitors of the tribes of Israel, named after the sons.

What Is This Story About?

Joseph's brothers, already resentful of their father's favoritism toward Joseph, were angry that he, second youngest, dreamed of being over the others. (Dreams were considered prophetic.) The brothers plotted to kill Joseph. Reuben, trying to save Joseph's life, suggested that they leave him in a pit rather than killing him themselves. By the time Reuben returned to rescue Joseph, the others had sold him. Judah figured they might as well make a profit. Perhaps Judah had found another way to preserve Joseph's life. The brothers did not tell Jacob the truth of what they'd done, saying that Joseph was dead. Jacob was inconsolable.

Why Is This Story Important?

What will become of Joseph? Sold by his brothers to the Midianites, they in turn sold Joseph in Egypt to the captain of Pharaoh's guard. What will become of the brothers who committed such evil against Joseph? Will Jacob ever learn what really happened? Will Joseph's dreams prove true? The Bible is full of dramatic stories. Each of us knows the realities of family power struggles, favoritism, love, hate, and violence. These realities go far beyond families, affecting even international relations. In the end (Genesis 45), God brought peace even to Jacob's family as God works for peace among all people.

Age-Level Connection

Young children—as well as adults!—often have a hard time making sense of dreams. And sometimes as they tell the adults in their lives something that may have happened to them, truth and fiction intertwine. In a child's mind, dreams are either good or bad. To a child, dreams happen when we are asleep. Reassure the children that God is always with us, night or day, when we are awake or asleep. And sometimes God does speak to people in their dreams.

Teacher Prayer

Dear God, sometimes I don't know which way to turn! I wish I could hear your voice more clearly, guiding me in the right direction. Help me to take the time to listen for the small voice that you sometimes use to speak! Amen

Question for Reflection

How does God speak to you?

Learner Goals

KNOW

God can speak to us in many ways, even in dreams

GROW

in understanding that God wants us to love our families

SHOW

love to family and friends

FACTOID

The Bible includes a variety of family arrangements, including polygamy, as in this story.

Ready for the Story (15 minutes)

Witness WORDS

dream, robe, wisdom

FACTOID

Hebron and Shechem were approximately 45 miles (72 km) apart. Hebron was south of Jerusalem; Shechem was north. Dothan was located about 15 miles (24 km) farther north of Shechem.

▶ **Transition Tip** ◀

Have the learners pretend to be sheep, following you and baaing as they move from the arrival time activities into the story circle.

Welcome the Witnesses

M&P *Locate the Witness CD from the Age 2–Grade 4 Teacher Class Kit (TCK) and a CD player. Put out the name tags for the children to put on as they arrive for class. If you have any new learners today, be sure to make a name tag for them as well.*

Play Track 3 of the CD as the children arrive and greet parents and caregivers as they drop their children off. **I am so excited to see you again this week! Sunday school is so much fun with all of you.**

Story Warm-Up

M&P *Gather an assortment of play farm animals, as well as a toy barn, people, and other toy farm equipment. A set of blocks would work with the animals if you don't have a barn.*

Show the learners the farm animals, farm equipment, and barn you have set up. Invite them to play with the animals and set up a farm. **Do any of you live on a farm? Have you visited a farm? Has anyone been to a petting zoo or a fair that has animals?** Allow time for learners to share. **How do you care for animals, especially on a farm? Who feeds the animals? Who gives them water? Who makes sure the animals stay healthy and are safe? In our Bible story today, Joseph helps take care of his family's animals. When you take care of sheep or goats, you are called a shepherd.**

Story Fire-Up

M&P *Display Poster O (TCK) where everyone can see it.*

Show learners the poster. **What do you think is happening in this poster?** *(Joseph is dreaming.)* **Do you ever dream? Do silly things ever happen in your dreams? Many stories in the Bible tell how God told people things in their dreams. God still talks to people in dreams today, but we may not know it. God talks to people in other ways too: through the words of the Bible, our families, our teachers or pastors, and our friends. Sometimes we just seem to know what God wants us to do. We call that wisdom.**

Explore the Story (20 minutes)

Story Set-Up

M&P *Gather Leaflet 3 from the Pre-Kindergarten/Kindergarten Learner Resource (LR) and the coat sticker from Sticker Sheet 2 (LR). Display Posters K and Q (TCK) and have the Session 3 Big Idea sentence strip from Activity Card D (TCK) and removable tape available. Remove the Session 2 sentence strip from the poster and display it somewhere in the classroom.*

Remind the learners that Joseph and his family had sheep and goats. **What do we call someone who takes care of sheep and goats?** *(A shepherd.)* **This poster shows some of the things a shepherd does. What things is the shepherd doing to care for the animals?** Ask for a volunteer to hand out the leaflets. Read the title aloud. Read about Joseph, his father, and his beautiful coat. Have the learners complete the picture of Joseph by placing the sticker of Joseph's coat on Joseph. Review the Sessions 1 and 2 Big Idea sentence strips displayed in the class. Look at the Big Idea printed on the back of the leaflet and read it aloud to the learners. **God knows we can do great things.** Invite a learner to tape the Session 3 Big Idea sentence strip to the space on the poster. Ask the learners to repeat this sentence with you, then have them turn to the person sitting next to them and repeat the words aloud together. **What kinds of great things can we do with God's help? Everything we do is great if God is helping us!**

Storytelling

M&P *You will need Leaflet 3 (LR) and simple props and costumes if you choose to dramatize the story.*

Ask the learners to open their leaflets and look at the left side. Point out the code at the bottom of the page and explain what each picture represents. Read the story of Joseph aloud as the learners follow along. Then read it aloud again, this time pausing at the rebus words—Joseph, brothers, sheep, dreams—so learners can say those words with you. To make the story really come alive, put out some simple props and costumes and invite the learners to act out the Bible story.

FAITH Traits

M&P *You will need the Session 3 Faith Trait sticker on Sticker Sheet 1 (LR), magnetic tape, each learner's poster board, and scissors.*

Today's Faith Trait is wisdom. Being wise means that you are smart and make good decisions. Do you know anyone who is wise? Have the learners attach the Faith Trait sticker to the poster board next to the space where they cut out the last piece. Help them cut the poster board around the shape of the sticker and attach a piece of magnetic tape to the back. Encourage learners to add this piece to their puzzle at home.

Kid Connect

Making good decisions is a learned behavior. None of us makes good decisions consistently without practice and experience. Giving learners opportunities to practice making good decisions can be an intentional part of a class routine, from choosing where to sit to making a good choice about participating in activities. Acknowledge learners who make good choices in your class.

More Movement

Invite the learners to practice being sheep and a shepherd. Because a shepherd leads his or her flock, play a game of Follow the Leader as sheep and a shepherd. Play enough times so everyone who wants to be a shepherd can lead the flock.

Teacher Boost

If teaching four-, five-, and six-year-olds is new to you, don't hesitate to check with other teachers who are familiar with this age if you are unsure of teaching techniques or tricks. There may be an experienced teacher in your congregation who could help with concerns you have and reassure you of all the things you are doing right.

Witnesses in the World

Sponsor a clothes drive for people in your community who are less fortunate. Make arrangements to collect warm clothes—such as coats, sweatshirts, and sweaters—that can be delivered to people who need them. Put announcements in the bulletin, newsletter, Web site, and on bulletin boards to let the congregation know about the drive and your class's involvement.

GREAT good byes

Make a special effort to give a hug or a kind word to each child as he or she leaves today.

Live the Story (25 minutes)

Ways to Witness

M&P *Each learner will need Leaflet 3 (LR) and crayons or markers.*

Have the learners turn to the next page in their leaflets. Point out the playground scene. **What do you notice about this picture?** *(There is a little girl who looks sad.)* **What do you think would help the little girl cheer up?** *(Accept learner responses.)* Point out the boy approaching the girl. **What should the boy do? Circle the picture that shows him making a good decision.** Allow learners time to complete the task. **Which picture did you circle? Why was that a good decision for the boy? What is one good decision you've made this week?**

Kids Create (Choose One!)

M&P *Rainbow Coats: Gather a large paper bag for each learner. Cut a coat shape from each bag as shown. Have crayons or markers available.*

Dream Streamers: Gather an embroidery hoop for each child. Cut 20" (51 cm) lengths of colorful ribbon for each learner to loop and tie around each hoop.

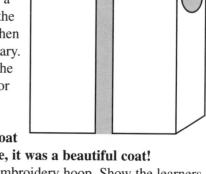

Rainbow Coats: Use the diagram to make a simple paper bag coat for each learner. Cut the basic shape into the paper bag beforehand, then adjust the coat shape to each child as necessary. Help each learner write his or her name on the back of the coat, then add strips, squiggles, or other designs with crayons or markers to decorate the coat. **You all have made such beautiful coats! I wonder what Joseph's coat looked like. If it looked anything like these, it was a beautiful coat!**
Dream Streamers: Give each learner an embroidery hoop. Show the learners how to fold a length of ribbon in half to make a loop, then lay the loop on the hoop and slip the two ends through the loop to fasten it to the hoop without knotting it. Have the learners fill their hoops with the ribbon. **These dream streamers can help remind you of Joseph's dreams.**

Wrapping It Up

M&P *Display Poster T (TCK).*

Ask the learners to gather their leaflets and any projects to take home and set them aside. Gather in a circle on the floor. Direct attention to the poster and point out that it shows kids doing great things. **What do you see kids doing here? Remember the Big Idea! Can you say it with me? God knows we can do great things. God spoke to Joseph in a dream, but God speaks to people in many different ways. We just need to listen!** Remind the learners about the fun things they can do at home that are printed on the back of the leaflet, and pray together. **Dear Lord, thank you for friends and family to love! Help us remember to share your love with everyone, and to listen carefully to you. Help us to make wise decisions in all we do and say. Amen**

Pharaoh's Dreams

Session at a Glance	What You Need	What Learners Do
Ready for the Story (15 minutes)		
Welcome the Witnesses	• Witness CD (TCK), CD player	• Listen to a CD.
Story Warm-Up	• Posters B and R (TCK), plastic construction blocks	• Look at a palace and Egyptian images, and build a city.
Story Fire-Up	• Posters P and R (TCK), books or pictures of Egyptian images	• Learn about what a pharaoh does, and about the Witness Words.
Explore the Story (20 minutes)		
Story Set-Up	• Leaflet 4 (LR), Activity Card D (TCK), Poster K (TCK), Reproducible Sheet C (TCK), removable tape, scissors, copier paper, crayons or markers	• Make crowns.
Storytelling	• Leaflet 4 (LR), Poster P (TCK)	• Hear the story of Pharaoh's dreams.
Faith Traits	• Sticker Sheet 1 (LR), magnetic tape, poster board, scissors	• Learn about the Faith Trait of stewardship.
Live the Story (25 minutes)		
Ways to Witness	• Leaflet 4 (LR), pen or pencil	• Think about ways to be a good steward.
Kids Create	• Blue construction paper, paper punch, gold or yellow yarn, scissors • Terra-cotta or plastic pots, puffy paints or other decorative paints, paint shirts, plants that root easily, plastic cups, permanent marker	• Make pocket pals. • Decorate pots and root plant cuttings.
Wrapping It Up	• Witness CD (TCK), CD player	• Review the Bible story.

Bible Text

Genesis 41:1-36

Key Verse

Joseph answered Pharaoh, "It is not I; God will give Pharaoh a favorable answer." Genesis 41:16

BIG Idea

God created enough for everyone.

LR = Learner Resource
TCK = Teacher Class Kit
M&P = Materials and Preparation

Teacher Prayer

Dear Lord, thank you for speaking to us in so many different ways. Help me learn to be a better listener. Amen

Question for Reflection

Would your family and friends say that you are a good listener?

Learner Goals

KNOW

they can help take care of God's world

GROW

in understanding good stewardship

SHOW

care for God's world

FACTOID

The Nile River is formed from the joining of the White Nile of Sudan and the Blue Nile of Ethiopia and flows north into the Mediterranean Sea.

Bible Background | ## What Factors Shaped This Story?

Pharaoh was the ruler over Egypt where the Midianites took Joseph and sold him into slavery. There Joseph, separated from his brothers, served as overseer in the house of Potiphar, one of Pharaoh's officers. Though innocent, Joseph was accused of a crime and put in prison (Genesis 39), where the inmates knew him as someone who could interpret dreams. It was considered important to interpret dreams, which were understood to be divine messages. For this reason, Pharaoh's court included magicians and wise men who might, among other things, interpret dreams. When they failed, the chief cupbearer remembered his experience with Joseph's ability to interpret dreams.

What Is This Story About?

Emerging from prison, Joseph was cleaned up and dressed for a meeting with Pharaoh. Joseph interpreted Pharaoh's troubling dreams, which told the same story. God was revealing to Pharaoh that seven years of famine would follow seven years of plenty. In his interpretation, Joseph not only pointed to God as the source of this message (41:25), he also acknowledged God as the source of his ability to interpret (41:16) and the source of the future predicted in the dream. Joseph went beyond interpretation. He advised Pharaoh with a plan to provide for the future. He told Pharaoh to set aside provisions during the plentiful years so there would be enough during the lean years.

Why Is This Story Important?

Pharaoh was willing to listen to a prisoner in the custody of the captain of the Egyptian guard. From the prisoner, he learned the meaning of his dreams and God's intent. Joseph pointed to God in the dreams, in his interpretation, and in the future unfolding. He also pointed to human beings' role in working with God. Rather than simply resigning himself to the coming famine, Joseph advised Pharaoh to plan for it. Think of the wealth of Pharaoh and Egypt, particularly in those plentiful years. An abundance of resources allowed the nation to set aside a fifth of the produce of the land and still have enough.

Age-Level Connection

Four-, five-, and six-year-olds love to think about being kings or queens and living in a castle. Think about ways to share with the learners that as children of God, we are children of the king.

Ready for the Story (15 minutes)

Welcome the Witnesses

M&P *Play Track 4 of the Witness CD from the Age 2–Grade 4 Teacher Class Kit (TCK) as the learners arrive.*

Welcome each learner by name. Give a special welcome to any guests or newly registered children, and make sure that at least two other children know their names. **Welcome back to Sunday school! Have you all had a good week?**

Story Warm-Up

M&P *Have available plastic construction blocks. Display Posters B and R (TCK) near the block area where everyone can see them.*

Show the learners the building blocks, and invite them to build a city with city walls and a palace. Point out the poster of the palace and the Egyptian images that are displayed in this area. **Today we're going to learn more about Joseph, the man we learned about last time. We'll learn about how Joseph helped a king from Egypt who lived in a palace!**

Story Fire-Up

M&P *Display Posters P and R (TCK) in the area where you will tell the story. If you have any books or pictures of Egyptian art or the pyramids, bring them to class.*

Show learners Poster P. **The word *pharaoh* is another word for "king." A pharaoh was a king in Egypt.** Point out Poster R that shows images and symbols of Egyptian art, and share any books or pictures you may have with pictures of the pyramids or other Egyptian artifacts. **Today's Bible story is about this pharaoh's dreams. What kinds of things does a king do?** After the learners share their thoughts and ideas, talk about the Witness Words for today. Explain what these words mean. **Stewardship means we take care of something. We can practice good stewardship by taking care of God's world. A drought is when there is little or no water for a long time. A famine is when there is little or no food for a long time. Sometimes after a drought, when there isn't enough rain for crops to grow, there is a famine.**

WORDS

stewardship, drought, famine

FACTOID

A pharaoh was a ruler of Egypt. Some of the pharaohs' names were Thutmose, Amenhotep, Tutankhamen (King Tut), Sety, and Rameses.

▶ **Transition Tip** ◀

Make sure to allow time for the learners to clean up their block city before moving on to the story.

Kid Connect

Many children are aware of stewardship, though they may not know it by that term. Young children have always lived in a world in which recycling and environmental issues are prominent. They can eagerly share the things they do at home or at school to recycle and take care of the earth. Help them to see that as people of God, this is an important task and something they are already good at doing!

More Movement

Use the Witness CD (TCK) as a springboard for movement during this part of the session. Young children need a break every 10 to 15 minutes. Make sure to include a game or activity that involves stretching, hand clapping, or movement of some kind. You can play the recycling game from Session 1 (page 9).

Explore the Story (20 minutes)

Story Set-Up

M&P *Gather Leaflet 4 from the Pre-Kindergarten/Kindergarten Learner Resource (LR). Display Poster K (TCK) and have the Session 4 Big Idea sentence strip from Activity Card D (TCK) and removable tape available. Remove the Session 3 sentence strip from the poster and display it somewhere in the classroom. Copy Reproducible Sheet C (TCK) for each child. Cut extra strips of copier paper to add to the crowns so they will fit around the learners' heads. Have crayons or markers and scissors available.*

Give each learner a crown to color and cut out. **We are all children of the king—God!** Offer help as needed as the children cut their crowns out. You may need to add extra strips of paper to the crowns with tape. Help the learners fit the crowns to their heads, and fasten securely. After the learners have finished their crowns, hand out the leaflets. Invite the learners to look at the front of the leaflet. Read the instructions and give them time to complete the dot-to-dot. Review the Sessions 1-3 Big Idea sentence strips displayed in the classroom. Point out the Big Idea printed on the back of the leaflet and read it aloud to the learners. Ask the learners to repeat it with you. **God created enough for everyone.** Invite a learner to tape the Session 4 Big Idea sentence strip to the space on the poster. **God provides everything we need!**

Storytelling

M&P *The learners need their Leaflet 4 (LR). Display Poster P (TCK) where everyone can see it.*

Ask the learners to open their leaflets and examine the Bible story art together. **Are there things in the picture that are similar to the poster of Egyptian art that we looked at?** Read the story aloud to the learners, having them point to any symbols or items in the Bible art as you mention them in the story. After reading the story, talk about the Witness Words *(stewardship, drought, famine)* and what they meant for the people living in the time of the pharaoh. **How did Joseph help Pharaoh? How did God help Joseph? What wise man did Pharaoh choose to help plan for the drought and famine that were going to come?**

FAITH Traits

M&P *You will need the Session 4 Faith Trait sticker on Sticker Sheet 1 (LR), magnetic tape, each learner's poster board, and scissors.*

The Faith Trait for today is stewardship. To be a good steward means to take good care of the earth. Have the learners attach the Faith Trait sticker to the poster board next to the space where they cut out their last piece. Help them cut the poster board around the shape of the sticker and attach a piece of magnetic tape to the back. Encourage learners to add this piece to their puzzle at home.

Live the Story *(25 minutes)*

Ways to Witness

M&P *The learners need their Leaflet 4 (LR).*

After hearing the Bible story, ask the learners to turn to the next page in their leaflets. Read aloud the title on the page: "How Can I Help?" **What does it mean to be helpful? How can we help others? What does it mean to be a good steward, or someone who takes care of something? How do you take care of your toys or books? Your pets? Your friends?** Have the learners look at the picture of the park where people have not been good stewards. **How could we be good stewards of this park?** Encourage the learners to share their ideas. Ask each child to think of a way she or he could help, and write that in her or his leaflet.

Kids Create (Choose One!)

M&P *Pocket Pals: Make a jeans pocket pattern using the diagram at right. Cut two "pockets" from blue construction paper for each learner. Place the two pieces together and punch holes on the sides and bottom. Cut lengths of gold or yellow yarn and tie two pocket pieces together on one end. Make a sample pocket by lacing through the holes to hold the pockets together.*

Growing Things: Each child will need a small, empty terra-cotta or plastic pot, a plant that roots easily in water (such as ivy or philodendron), and a plastic cup. Also have puffy paints or other decorative paints, paint shirts, and a permanent marker available.

Pocket Pals: Show the learners the sample pocket pal you made, and give them their own set of pockets to stitch. Encourage them to sew the pockets together. As the learners stitch, talk about stewardship. **We can be good stewards of many things. This pocket pal can be a place to put money or important things that we want to take good care of.**

Growing Things: Have each child put on a paint shirt. Encourage learners to use the paints to decorate their pots. Show the plants you brought. **These plants will form roots if the cut ends are put in a cup of water.** Give several cuttings to each learner, and write their names on the plastic cups. Have the learners take their cup of cuttings and their decorated pots home. **Add water to your cup and put it in a lighted place. Once the roots form, add soil to your pots and plant the new plants to help make God's creation more beautiful.**

Wrapping It Up

M&P *Have available the Witness CD (TCK) and a CD player.*

Have the learners gather with you in a circle on the floor, setting aside the items they will take home with them. Play Track 4 of the CD as a review of the Bible story. Ask the learners to repeat the Big Idea for today. Remind them to show their families all of the fun things to do that are printed on the back of the leaflet, then ask the learners to hold hands in the circle and pray with you. **Dear Lord, thank you for friends! Thank you for this world and for creating enough for everyone. Help us find ways to make sure we are good stewards of all of your gifts. Amen**

Teacher Boost

Now that you have spent several sessions with these children, you are more familiar with their names and some of their interests. If you have a hard time remembering names, continue to have learners wear name tags. One of the most significant things we can do for others is to know their names!

Witnesses in the World

How does your congregation practice stewardship? How might your class or the entire Sunday school program help? Many world hunger organizations have great programs for children. Look on-line to find one that would work for your class. Gain support for your project from your congregation.

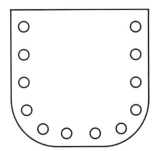

Go Global!

Check out the Session 4 Go Global! activity on Reproducible Sheets I and J (TCK). See page 3 of this guide.

Have each child wear his or her crown. **Good-bye, (child's name). Remember that you are a child of the king!** Remind each one to be a good steward this week.

The Ten Commandments

Bible Text

Exodus 20:1-17

Key Verse

You shall have no other gods before me. Exodus 20:3

God helps us do what is right.

Session at a Glance	What You Need	What Learners Do
Ready for the Story (20 minutes)		
Welcome the Witnesses	• Witness CD (TCK), CD player	• Listen to a CD.
Story Warm-Up	• Children's card games or board games	• Play games with simple rules.
Story Fire-Up	• Poster I (TCK)	• Learn about the Ten Commandments.
Explore the Story (15 minutes)		
Story Set-Up	• Leaflet 5 (LR), Sticker Sheet 2 (LR), Activity Card D (TCK), Poster K (TCK), removable tape, crayons or markers	• Complete a maze.
Storytelling	• Leaflet 5 (LR), Poster I (TCK), Witness CD (TCK), CD player	• Learn the story of how God gave us the Ten Commandments.
Faith Traits	• Sticker Sheet 1 (LR), magnetic tape, poster board, scissors	• Learn about the Faith Trait of obedience.
Live the Story (25 minutes)		
Ways to Witness	• Leaflet 5 (LR)	• Think about rules.
Kids Create	• Construction paper, scissors, crayons or markers • Poster I (TCK), 10 different colors of plastic or wooden beads, strong cord, key rings, scissors	• Make door hangers. • Make key chains.
Wrapping It Up	• Leaflet 5 (LR)	• Review Bible story and the Ten Commandments.

LR = Learner Resource
TCK = Teacher Class Kit
M&P = Materials and Preparation

What Factors Shaped This Story?

Liberated from slavery in Egypt, the ancient Israelites wandered in the wilderness. God had led them to freedom and continued to lead them in the wilderness until they arrived at Mount Sinai. There, through Moses, God reminded the people of their liberation and called on them to obey God, who had made them God's own people. One day God appeared on Mount Sinai in fire and smoke and in the sound of thunder. Moses brought out the people to meet God at the foot of the mountain. Only Moses and his brother Aaron were permitted on the top of the mountain.

What Is This Story About?

The Ten Commandments are God's words to shape a way of life that would help the liberated people remain free. God called on them to obey so they would remain God's "treasured possession out of all the peoples…a priestly kingdom and a holy nation" (19:5-6). The Commandments include laws about our relationship with God and our relationships with one another. They teach us to focus on God in worship, in possessions, and in use of language and time. They teach respect for others' lives, relationships, possessions, and names. Biblical interpreters and scholars number the Commandments differently, depending on whether 20:4-6 or 20:17 is counted as one or two commandments.

Why Is This Story Important?

The ancient Israelites knew Egyptian slavery as their way of life. Wilderness wandering helped them let go of that way of life. What would take its place? The Ten Commandments provided the basis of that new way of life. The people's life together in the presence of God who had liberated them would be a life of obedience and freedom. God's will for them was freedom, but they would not stay free if they did not obey. In the face of the human inclination to sin, God gave the people the gift of a way of life that would maintain their relationships with God and one another.

Age-Level Connection

Young children like to know what the rules or boundaries are. They may not always like them, but knowing rules or boundaries is a secure feeling. It is a relief for them to know what people's expectations are, and to know that the people who make the rules for them do so to keep them safe. Rules can make it fair for everyone. God's rules can be as reassuring for us.

Teacher Prayer

Dear Lord, sometimes I wonder if rules are a good thing! Does it really matter if I go a few miles above the speed limit or don't stop completely at a stop sign? Help me to keep in mind that the rules of society, and the Ten Commandments, are intended to help keep people safe. Thank you for loving me always, even at times when I don't follow the rules! Amen

Question for Reflection

Which is the hardest commandment to keep?

Learner Goals

KNOW

God gives us rules to help us live a good life

GROW

in understanding that God's rules are good for us

SHOW

kindness, courtesy, and respect to others

FACTOID

Mount Sinai is assumed to have been on today's Sinai Peninsula, which is bordered by the Mediterranean Sea and the Gulfs of Suez and Aqaba.

Ready for the Story (20 minutes)

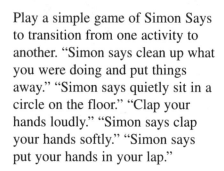

Witness WORDS

obedience, commandment, rule

FACTOID

An idol is something human-made and worshiped as representing a god. Idols symbolize an object of worship.

▶ Transition Tip ◀

Play a simple game of Simon Says to transition from one activity to another. "Simon says clean up what you were doing and put things away." "Simon says quietly sit in a circle on the floor." "Clap your hands loudly." "Simon says clap your hands softly." "Simon says put your hands in your lap."

Welcome the Witnesses

M&P *Have the Witness CD from the Age 2–Grade 4 Teacher Class Kit (TCK) playing as the learners arrive, especially Tracks 1-4, which reflect Bible stories the children have heard.*

Welcome learners by name and greet parents or caregivers as they drop their children off. **Good morning! How are you today?**

Story Warm-Up

M&P *You will need assorted children's board or card games, such as Go Fish, Candy Land, or Hi Ho! Cherry-O.*

As learners arrive, alternate by their arrival times where they will sit and which game they will play. If you have chosen simple games such as those suggested, you may not need to give directions about how to play the game. If there are questions, review the game rules with the learners as they begin to play. Try to allow time for at least one game to be completed before ending this portion of the session.

Story Fire-Up

M&P *Display Poster I (TCK) where everyone can see it.*

After the learners have completed at least one game and cleaned it up, gather together and show them the poster you have displayed. **Do you know what the Ten Commandments are?** *(Allow time for answers.)* **This poster shows us the Ten Commandments—rules that God gave to Moses to share with the people. Do you know one of the Ten Commandments?** *(Allow time for answers.)* Count from 1-10 on the poster, counting the Commandments with the learners and reading them aloud. **The Commandments God gave to Moses are for us today too. In our Bible story, we will learn more about the Commandments and what they are.** Tell the learners the Witness Words and explain what these words mean.

Explore the Story (20 minutes)

Story Set-Up

 M&P *Gather Leaflet 5 from the Pre-Kindergarten/Kindergarten Learner Resource (LR) and the Moses sticker from Sticker Sheet 2 (LR). Display Poster K (TCK) and have the Session 5 Big Idea sentence strip from Activity Card D (TCK), removable tape, and crayons or markers available. Remove the Session 4 sentence strip from the poster and display it somewhere in the classroom.*

Invite a learner to hand out the leaflets and look together at the front. Point out the maze that goes up the mountain. Read the instructions for this page aloud, then give each learner a Moses sticker to put at the bottom of the mountain. Have them complete the maze that will help Moses find his way up the mountain. Review the Sessions 1-4 Big Idea sentence strips that have been presented so far, using the sentence strips you have displayed in the classroom. Point out the Big Idea printed on the back of the leaflet. **God helps us do what is right.** Invite a learner to tape the Big Idea sentence strip to the space on the poster. **How does God help us to do what is right?**

Storytelling

M&P *The learners need Leaflet 5 (LR). Display Poster I (TCK) where you will be telling the Bible story. Listen to Track 5 on the Witness CD (TCK) and begin to learn this rhythmic way of memorizing the Ten Commandments.*

Ask the learners to open their leaflets. Examine the Bible story picture on the left with the learners, and ask them to count the number of Commandments aloud with you. Read the story, spending time on the explanation of what a commandment—or rule—is. Invite the learners to count the Commandments. Listen to Track 5 on the CD and encourage learners to begin to memorize the Ten Commandments. **How many of you have rules to follow at home or at school? If you are on a sports team, are there rules you need to follow? What kinds of rules are there? God's rules—or commandments—are good for us to follow today, just as they were for the Israelites.** Use examples the learners give, such as rules for a sports team or family rules, to help them understand how rules can help us to stay safe, to play fair, and to live like God wants us to.

FAITH Traits

M&P *You will need the Session 5 Faith Trait sticker on Sticker Sheet 1 (LR), magnetic tape, each learner's poster board, and scissors.*

Today's Faith Trait is obedience. What does it mean to obey? When we obey God, or follow God's rules or commandments, we know we're doing what is right. Remind them of the Big Idea. **God helps us do what is right. Sometimes it isn't easy to do the right thing, but God will always help us.** Have the learners attach the Faith Trait sticker to the poster board next to the space where they cut out their last piece. Help them cut the poster board around the shape of the sticker and attach a piece of magnetic tape to the back. Encourage learners to add this piece to their puzzle at home.

Kid Connect

Children this age are very much aware of right and wrong. In their minds, things tend to be all or nothing, with no degrees in between. At times they may seem overly interested in fairness issues, and telling on others—tattling— can be a problem. Explain to the learners that tattling to get others in trouble is not all right.

More Movement

Play a game that has simple rules, such as Red Light, Green Light or Mother, May I? Both games are good for moving, but also emphasize the fact that rules are an important part of playing the game.

Teacher Boost

Are you enjoying this age group? They certainly have their quirks and challenges, but they are eager to learn and love God! What is a better combination than that?

Witnesses in the World

How can your class help with some of the maintenance chores around the church building? Check with the church office for some routine jobs that you might take on, such as folding bulletins or handing them out at worship, collecting used bulletins for recycling, or wiping wet counters in the bathroom.

GREAT good byes

Review the Ten Commandments using Track 5 of the Witness CD (TCK). Give every child a "high ten" as he or she leaves class today.

Live the Story (25 minutes)

Story Follow-Up

M&P *Each learner will need Leaflet 5 (LR).*

Have learners look at the pictures on the next page of the leaflet, and ask volunteers to describe the pictures to you. **Are any of these people not following the rules?** Read the directions for this activity aloud, and show the learners how to put an X through the illustrations that show someone breaking the rules. **Are some rules harder to follow than other rules? What kinds of rules are hard to follow?**

Kids Create (Choose One!)

M&P *Ten Commandments Door Hangers: Use the diagram below to trace a door hanger on construction paper, one for each child. Have crayons or markers and scissors available.*

Ten-Bead Chains: You will need 10 different colored plastic or wooden beads for each learner, strong cord, and key rings. Display Poster I (TCK) in the work area.

Ten Commandments Door Hangers: Give each learner a door hanger you traced and encourage them to cut it out. Offer help as necessary. **Decorate your door hangers with images that remind you of the Ten Commandments, such as hugging your parents or singing in church. It is important to learn the Ten Commandments and to try to follow them all of our lives. Ten-Bead Chains:** Have each learner collect ten beads, one of each color. Show how to thread the beads onto the cord, helping them to tie a knot between each bead. Tie a strong knot on either end so the beads do not fall off the cord. Attach the 10-bead chain to the key ring. **Each bead can be for one of the Ten Commandments to help you remember them!**

Wrapping It Up

Gather the learners together, setting aside any items they will take home with them. Review the Bible story about the Ten Commandments, as well as the Faith Trait and Big Idea. **God gave us the Ten Commandments so we would know what was right and obey God's rules. You did a great job of obeying the rules and doing what is right today!** Review the Witness Words and talk about how we can be obedient in our lives as God's children. Point out the fun activities printed on the back of the leaflet, and ask the learners to hold hands for prayer. Ask if there is anyone who would like to pray a prayer of thanks to God. Close by adding: **Thank you, God, for all of my friends in this class! Amen**

David Is Anointed

Session at a Glance	What You Need	What Learners Do
Ready for the Story (15 minutes)		
Welcome the Witnesses	• Witness CD (TCK), CD player	• Listen to a CD.
Story Warm-Up	• Heart-shaped cookies, paper, envelopes, pen	• Eat a cookie and read a special message about themselves.
Story Fire-Up	• Chart paper, crayons or markers	• Discover their God-given gifts through others' insights.
Explore the Story (20 minutes)		
Story Set-Up	• Leaflet 6 (LR), Sticker Sheet 2 (LR), Activity Card D (TCK), Poster K (TCK), removable tape, crayons or markers	• Find the hidden sheep.
Storytelling	• Leaflet 6 (LR), Witness CD (TCK), CD player	• Learn the story of how David was chosen by God.
Faith Traits	• Sticker Sheet 1 (LR), magnetic tape, poster board, scissors	• Learn about the Faith Trait of humility.
Live the Story (25 minutes)		
Ways to Witness	• Leaflet 6 (LR), Poster T (TCK), crayons or markers	• Discover that God has chosen them.
Kids Create	• White construction paper, washable red paint, paintbrushes, paint shirts, crayons or markers, hand wipes or warm soapy water and paper towels • Cardboard picture frames, markers, embellishments, glue	• Make heart handprints. • Make "God Made Me Special" frames.
Wrapping It Up	• Bible	• Review the Bible story.

Bible Text

1 Samuel 16

Key Verse

The Lord looks on the heart.
1 Samuel 16:7

Anyone can be called to serve God.

LR = Learner Resource
TCK = Teacher Class Kit
M&P = Materials and Preparation

Teacher Prayer

Thank you, Lord, for choosing me to teach these young members of your family! Guide my preparation and planning and my words and actions as I spend time with these learners. Help me to be a role model for them, living out your love in all I say and do. Amen

Question for Reflection

Besides teaching, how are you called to serve God?

Learner Goals

KNOW

God chooses each of us to do something special for God

GROW

in understanding God's loving care for them

SHOW

loving service to others

FACTOID

Saul, ancient Israel's first king, ruled approximately 1020 to 1000 B.C. He was a descendant of Jacob's youngest son Benjamin. *Saul* means "asked for."

Bible Background **What Factors Shaped This Story?**

Samuel had been consecrated to God at an early age. When he was serving in the temple under the priest, Eli, God called Samuel to be a prophet. The ancient Israelites had only God as their sovereign. Wanting to be like the other nations of the world, the people went to Samuel demanding a king to govern them. Samuel took this request to God, who warned that having an earthly king would lead the people into slavery. The people refused to listen to Samuel when he told them God's response, so God gave them Saul to be their king. Saul sinned in his leadership of the people and was rejected by God.

What Is This Story About?

God sent Samuel to anoint a new king to replace Saul. Samuel went to Jesse and his sons in Bethlehem. He pretended to be there to make a sacrifice so Saul would not suspect his mission and try to kill him. Jesse and seven of his eight sons joined Samuel at his sacrifice. All seven sons seemed likely candidates, but none was the one whom God would designate king. God reminded Samuel that God does not see as humans see but looks at people's hearts, not at their outward appearance. Jesse's eighth son, David, who had been tending sheep, was the one. Samuel anointed him, putting oil on his head.

Why Is This Story Important?

God responded to the people's desire and provided a king in Saul. When Saul proved unfit, God provided another king. Obedient to God, the prophet Samuel followed God's will in the selection and anointing of the new king, David. By outward appearances David did not seem the most likely of Jesse's sons to be king, but God's way of seeing was different from the way human beings see. God saw the heart of a person and chose David. God willed good for the people through their kings despite God's warning that having a king was a mistake.

Age-Level Connection

Four-, five-, and six-year-olds love to be chosen to be the helper or for special responsibilities. Even simple chores become fun when we are chosen specially to do them. Make a point to include each child as a special helper during this semester. You may want to alternate helpers throughout the session or choose a different person each week. Either way, each child will appreciate being chosen!

Ready for the Story (15 minutes)

Welcome the Witnesses

M&P *Play the Witness CD from the Age 2–Grade 4 Teacher Class Kit (TCK) as the learners arrive.*

Welcome learners by name and greet any parents or caregivers who drop off their children, thanking them for doing so each week. **Welcome back! I'm so glad to see all of you today!**

Story Warm-Up

M&P *Make or purchase heart-shaped cookies for the learners. Note: Before serving any food, always check with caregivers for learners who have food allergies. Provide an alternative if necessary. Write a special message on a piece of paper, commenting on something special or unique about each child. Put each message in an envelope with the child's name on it and lay each envelope and a cookie on the table.*

Invite each child to sit at the place with his or her name and enjoy the cookie. After everyone arrives, tell the learners they can open the envelopes with their names on them and see what the message says. Walk around to help the children read their messages. **I am so glad that God made each of you special!**

Story Fire-Up

M&P *Print "Chosen by God" at the top of a sheet of chart paper and each child's name under the heading. Display the poster on the wall.*

You are special children of God, and God loves you very much! Talk about the ways that we are all special and unique, not just in the way that we look, but in all of the things we like to do. Take time to share at least one comment about each child in the group, such as: *(Child's name)* **is a great soccer player.** *(Child's name)* **sings beautifully.** Encourage the learners to think of something nice about each person in the class, and have them take turns sharing with the class their "something nice" about a classmate.

Witness WORDS

humility, serve, anointed

FACTOID

Because Joseph was descended from David, Mary and Joseph traveled to Bethlehem from Nazareth for the census. Jesus was born in Bethlehem, located 6 miles (10 km) south of Jerusalem.

 Transition Tip

Use something unique in every person—such as eye color—as a transition method today. When you change activities, ask first for those with brown eyes, then blue, then green, and so on.

Children this age are self-centered. They are just beginning to learn that the world does not revolve around them. Help them learn this concept by encouraging them to share with one another, to take turns, and to try to treat other people in the way that they would like to be treated.

More Movement

Hide toy sheep or sheep cutouts around the class. Let the learners pretend they are shepherds and need to find their lost sheep.

Explore the Story (20 minutes)

Story Set-Up

M&P *Gather Leaflet 6 from the Pre-Kindergarten/Kindergarten Learner Resource (LR). Display Poster K (TCK) and have the Session 6 Big Idea sentence strip from Activity Card D (TCK), removable tape, and crayons or markers available. Remove the Session 5 sentence strip from the poster and display it somewhere in the classroom.*

Invite a learner to help you hand out the leaflets. **Look at the front page of your leaflet. This is a hidden picture.** Read the directions about David. **David needs to find all the hidden sheep! Can you help him?** Have the learners circle all the hidden sheep in the picture. **How many sheep are there? Let's count together to find out!** Count the sheep aloud. *(There are four hidden sheep.)* Review the Sessions 1-5 Big Idea sentence strips, using the sentence strips you have displayed. Now read the Big Idea printed on the back of the leaflet aloud. **Anyone can be called to serve God.** Choose a learner to tape the Big Idea sentence strip to the space on the poster. **What does "called to serve God" mean? Does God call people on the telephone? When people talk about being called to do something, it means that they feel God wants them to do it, that God has a purpose for them. Many pastors or people who work in churches feel called. We are all called to serve God in many different ways.** Share ways you feel God has called you, and help the learners understand that even though they are children, they are called to serve God too. Review the Big Idea together and have the learners repeat this concept with you several times.

Storytelling

M&P *Have Leaflet 6 (LR) available. Preview Track 6 of the Witness CD (TCK), and decide whether you will use this version of the story presentation or if you will read the Bible story as presented in the leaflet.*

Ask the learners to open their leaflets. **Look at the Bible story picture on the left. David was a shepherd as a boy but later he was chosen by God to become a king.** Read the story of David from the leaflet aloud or use Track 6 of the CD to present it. **Although David was young, God still called him to do great things.**

FAITH Traits

M&P *You will need the Session 6 Faith Trait sticker on Sticker Sheet 1 (LR), magnetic tape, each learner's poster board, and scissors.*

Review all of the Faith Traits you have learned so far. **Today's Faith Trait is humility. When we are humble or have humility, we don't think we are better than anyone else. We know God made us special, just as everyone is special, and we can do great things for God!** Have the learners attach the Faith Trait sticker to the poster board next to the space where they cut out their last piece. Help them cut the poster board around the shape of the sticker and attach a piece of magnetic tape to the back. Encourage learners to add this piece to their puzzle at home.

Live the Story (25 minutes)

Ways to Witness

M&P *Each learner will need Leaflet 6 (LR) and crayons or markers. Display Poster T (TCK) where everyone can see it.*

Read aloud "Who Does God Choose Today?" printed at the top of the next page of the leaflet. **God still chooses people today. Who are some people that God chooses to do great things?** Invite ideas from the learners. **God chooses you to do things too! What are some things God has chosen you to do?** Allow time for answers. Encourage learners to draw themselves in the frame on the page. Point out the poster. **What are some of the great things the kids on the poster are doing?**

Kids Create (Choose One!)

M&P *Heart Handprints: You will need 9" x 12" (23 cm x 30 cm) white construction paper for each learner. Make sure to have red paint that will wash off hands easily. It is best to paint each learner's hands with a paintbrush. If a sink isn't available, have a dishpan of soapy water or hand wipes for cleaning up. Gather paint shirts. Make a sample heart handprint.*

"God Made Me Special" Frames: You will need one simple cardboard picture frame for each learner. Print "God Made Me Special" on each frame, one word on each side. Gather markers and embellishments the learners can glue to the frames to decorate them, such as buttons, small pom-poms, or foam pieces.

 Heart Handprints: Have learners put on paint shirts. To make a heart with hands, paint the entire palm, then press the painted hand onto a piece of white construction paper. Paint the other hand and press it onto the paper, overlapping the first handprint as shown and forming the shape of a heart. Help the learners print their names at the bottom of the prints. **God looks at our hearts. Now your family and friends can look at these beautiful hearts you have made!**

"God Made Me Special" Frames: Give each learner a frame. Encourage them to decorate the frame with markers and buttons or other embellishments that you have provided. **Hang this frame in a special place in your room and put your own picture in it to remind you that you are chosen by God!**

Wrapping It Up

M&P *Have a Bible available.*

Gather together in a circle. Review today's Bible story, Big Idea, and Faith Trait. Read aloud the Key Verse, 1 Samuel 16:7, from your Bible. **All people who love God are called to share the good news of God's love with others. How can we serve God and others at home, at school, and while we play?** Remind the learners of the fun activities to do with their families on the back of their leaflets. Pray the following prayer to the tune of "Are You Sleeping?" Encourage learners to fill in the blanks with things for which they are thankful. **Thank you, God! Thank you, God! / For our _____! For our _____! / We will always love you. We will always share you. / Thank you, God! Thank you, God!**

Teacher Boost

Choosing a child as a helper is a good way to make him or her feel special and recognized. Note on your attendance chart or on a note card clipped to your teacher guide which children have been chosen. This will ensure that everyone will have a chance to help.

Witnesses in the World

Ask the children how they could best serve their families at home. **What can you do at home to help your families?** Offer a few ideas to get them started, such as feeding a pet without being asked, collecting the trash on trash day, setting the table, hanging up wet towels, or helping with the grocery shopping.

GREAT good byes

Give each child a special smile as you say good-bye. Let them know you are glad they were here today, and you look forward to seeing them again next time.

Solomon's Dream

Bible Text

1 Kings 3:3-15

Key Verse

Solomon loved the Lord.
1 Kings 3:1

Wisdom comes from God.

Session at a Glance	What You Need	What Learners Do
Ready for the Story (15 minutes)		
Welcome the Witnesses	• Witness CD (TCK), CD player	• Listen to a CD.
Story Warm-Up	• Red and green construction paper, scissors	• Discern between true and false statements.
Story Fire-Up	• Nothing.	• Play a game of Telephone.
Explore the Story (20 minutes)		
Story Set-Up	• Leaflet 7 (LR), Sticker Sheet 2 (LR), Activity Card D (TCK), Poster K (TCK), removable tape	• Learn about Solomon's dream.
Storytelling	• Leaflet 7 (LR), Witness CD (TCK), CD player	• Hear the story of Solomon's dream.
Faith Traits	• Sticker Sheet 1 (LR), magnetic tape, poster board, scissors	• Learn about the Faith Trait of wisdom.
Live the Story (25 minutes)		
Ways to Witness	• Leaflet 7 (LR), crayons or markers	• Discover what God gave to Solomon.
Kids Create	• White construction paper, washable paint, paintbrushes, paint shirts, markers, hand wipes or water and paper towels • Key rings, leather strips or yarn, scissors, alphabet and heart beads	• Make "Love the Lord" banners. • Make name key chains.
Wrapping It Up	• Witness CD (TCK), CD player, Bible	• Review the Bible story.

LR = Learner Resource
TCK = Teacher Class Kit
M&P = Materials and Preparation

Bible Background — What Factors Shaped This Story?

David was ancient Israel's second king. He chose his son Solomon to succeed him. After a political struggle with David's oldest surviving son, Adonijah, over who would become king, Solomon was made king. For a time Solomon dealt peacefully with Adonijah but the rivalry between them did not go away. To consolidate his power, Solomon killed not only Adonijah but those who had supported him and others who had been David's enemies. His reign established, Solomon married a daughter of Pharaoh to make an alliance with the king of Egypt.

What Is This Story About?

Solomon followed in his father David's footsteps as a king who walked with God and pleased God. In a dream God appeared to Solomon, asking him what to give him. Solomon was in awe at the task of following David as king, a faithful and righteous leader, beloved of God. Solomon did not ask for wealth or fame, for military victory or long life. Solomon asked God for wisdom in governing the people and in discerning between good and evil. Pleased with Solomon's response, God granted his request and promised Solomon incomparable riches and honor and, if Solomon kept God's commandments, long life.

Why Is This Story Important?

Among the ancient Israelites, dreams were one way God communicated with people. Solomon's dream was a way for God to speak to Solomon and for Solomon to speak to God. The dream revealed his heart's desire and his anxiety at being king, particularly following such a great king as David. The dream also revealed God's reassuring response to Solomon and God's intent for Solomon. God answered Solomon's dream prayer for wisdom. God responded with more than Solomon asked because Solomon's prayer was for a gift that pleased God and would equip Solomon to walk in God's ways.

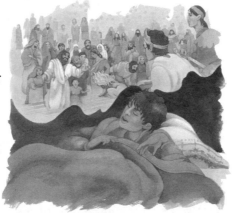

Age-Level Connection

Making decisions is an important part of being a child. It is not something that comes naturally or easily to a young child. It's a learned process. Find ways to help develop this ability in the learners. For example, offer them specific choices ("Would you like to use a red marker or a blue marker?") rather than questions without choices ("Would you like to color this picture?").

Teacher Prayer

Dear Lord, thank you for questions to ask and for answers given. Help me to always look to you first for times when I need wisdom in my life. Amen

Question for Reflection

Who is the wisest person you know?

Learner Goals

KNOW

God gives wisdom

GROW

in understanding that God speaks to us through other people and the Bible

SHOW

wisdom in making choices in daily life

FACTOID

Burnt offerings are one form of sacrifice described in the Bible. Another is offering slaughtered whole animals or animal parts, often fat or blood.

WITNESS WORDS

wisdom, justice, govern

FACTOID

God warned against having a king (1 Samuel 8:10-19). Solomon established a temple, a palace, and an army. Forced labor helped pay for them.

▶ Transition Tip ◀

Use the learners' birthdays as a way of making transitions today. Ask the learners to raise their hands if they're four years old. How many are five? How many are six? Whenever you make a transition from one activity to another today, ask the four-year-olds to make the change, then the five-year-olds, then the six-year-olds. Alternate the ages so the learners don't stop listening to you!

Ready for the Story (15 minutes)

Welcome the Witnesses

M&P *Play the Witness CD from the Age 2–Grade 4 Teacher Class Kit (TCK) as the learners gather.*

Welcome learners, as well as guests, by name. Thank the parents and caregivers for bringing their children today. **Good morning, everyone! How was your week?**

Story Warm-Up

M&P *Cut red and green construction paper into 3" x 5" (8 cm x 13 cm) cards. Each learner will need one red and one green card.*

Give each learner a set of red and green cards and tell them that these are "True" and "False" cards. **Who knows what true and false mean?** Encourage learners to share their ideas. **Something that is correct is true. Something that is wrong or incorrect is false. I'm going to say some things or ask some questions that could be true or false. Listen carefully to what I say and hold up the green card if you think what I say is true, or hold up the red card if you think what I say is false.** Give some statements that have a definite true or false answer (such as "The sun is in the sky" or "Snakes have legs"). Say several, then let any learners who would wish to make up true and false statements do so. Play for a few minutes. **We know some of these things are true and others are false. How do we know?**

Story Fire-Up

M&P *Before playing this game, be aware of any children who have a hearing loss and adjust the game accordingly.*

Have the learners form a circle. **We're going to play a game of Telephone. I'll whisper a message into the ear of** *(the child sitting on your right)* **and** *(child's name)* **will whisper the message** *(he or she)* **heard to the next person. We'll keep doing that until the message has gone all the way around the circle. The last person will tell us the message** *(he or she)* **heard.** Was it the same as the message you started? **Let's try this again to see if we can become better listeners if we concentrate.**

Explore the Story (20 minutes)

Story Set-Up

M&P *Gather Leaflet 7 from the Pre-Kindergarten/Kindergarten Learner Resource (LR) and the Solomon sticker from Sticker Sheet 1 (LR). Display Poster K (TCK) and have the Session 7 Big Idea sentence strip from Activity Card D (TCK) and removable tape available. Remove the Session 6 sentence strip from the poster and display it somewhere in the classroom.*

Invite a learner to help you hand out the leaflets. Look at the front together. **These pictures show things that Solomon could have asked God for. Add the sticker of Solomon dreaming at the bottom of the page. Solomon could have asked God for all of these things but he asked God for something different. Solomon asked God for wisdom. We learned about wisdom a few weeks ago. Who remembers what** *wisdom* **means?** Allow time for answers, and explain what wisdom means, if necessary. Read the Big Idea, found on the back of the leaflet, aloud. **Wisdom comes from God. God can speak to us in many ways, and sometimes God gives us wisdom through the words of other people, the Bible, and things that happen in our lives.** Invite a learner to tape the Big Idea sentence strip to the space on the poster. Then have everyone shout together: **Wisdom comes from God!**

Storytelling

M&P *Make sure each learner has Leaflet 7 (LR). Listen to Track 7 of the Witness CD (TCK) to decide whether you would like to introduce the Bible story using this song.*

Have the learners open their leaflets and look at the Bible story picture on the left. Read the Key Verse aloud. **Because Solomon loved the Lord, God wanted to reward him. When God asked Solomon what he wanted, God was pleased with Solomon's answer.** Read the Bible story printed in the leaflet aloud. **Because Solomon asked for wisdom, God rewarded him with riches and a long life.** Remind the learners about the Big Idea.

FAITH Traits

M&P *You will need the Session 7 Faith Trait sticker on Sticker Sheet 1 (LR), magnetic tape, each learner's poster board, and scissors.*

Review the Faith Traits the learners have learned so far. **Today's Faith Trait is wisdom.** Have the learners attach the Faith Trait sticker to the poster board next to the space where they cut out their last piece. Help them cut the poster board around the shape of the sticker and attach a piece of magnetic tape to the back. Encourage learners to add this piece to their puzzle at home.

Kid Connect

All people like to be acknowledged for the good things they do. As you notice children making wise or kind decisions or choices in class, acknowledge them by saying something such as, "*(Child's name)*, it was nice of you to help *(another child's name)* pick up the crayons *(he or she)* dropped," or "*(Child's name)*, thank you for helping me clean up the blocks, even though you weren't playing with them!" or "That was a wise decision!"

More Movement

Play a game of Simon Says as a movement game today. **Listening and following directions is a large part of this game, not just being able to do what you think Simon wants you to do. So really try to listen to everything!**

Teacher Boost

Learners can understand that most adults are wise and know more than children do. But adults don't know everything. If a child asks you a question and you don't know the answer, it's better to say, "I'm not sure" or "I don't know. Let's try to find out together." Children respect honesty more than someone trying to act as if he or she has all the answers.

Witnesses in the World

Making wise choices isn't easy for anyone. Help the children learn more about making some of these choices by role-playing situations they could find themselves in and talking through and acting out what they could do. **Your best friend cuts in front of someone in line to go outside and wants you to do it too. What do you do?**

Go Global!

Check out the Session 7 Go Global! activity on Reproducible Sheets I and J (TCK). See page 3 of this guide.

GREAT good byes

Give each child a high five as she or he leaves. **Be wise this week!**

Live the Story (25 minutes)

Story Follow-Up

M&P *Each learner will need Leaflet 7 (LR) and crayons or markers.*

Ask the learners to look at the next page in their leaflets. Explain the hidden word puzzle to the children. **Color any space that has a dot in it with your favorite color to discover what God gave to Solomon. God gives us lots of things, like families, wisdom, love, and talents. What things has God given you?**

Kids Create (Choose One!)

M&P *"Love the Lord" Banners: Each learner will need one 9" x 12" (23 cm x 30 cm) sheet of construction paper. Scallop one narrow end of each sheet. You will also need washable paint, paintbrushes, paint shirts, markers, and hand wipes or water and paper towels. Make a sample banner.*

Name Key Chains: You will need a length of leather or yarn (cut ahead of time in varying lengths to allow for shorter and longer names) and a key ring for each learner, enough alphabet beads to spell each learner's name, and two heart beads per learner. Before class, follow the directions below to make your own key chain to use as a sample.

"Love the Lord" Banners: Show the learners the sample banner you have made. Help them put on paint shirts, paint their hands, place their handprint in the center of the banner, and wash their hands. Write "*(Child's name)* loves the Lord!" on each banner. If you like, show the learners how to use a marker to make "stitches" around the edge of the paper banner to look like it was sewn. **Solomon loved God so much. You can hang this banner in your house to show your family how much you love God!**

Name Key Chains: Give each learner a key ring, a length of leather or yarn, two heart beads, and alphabet beads with letters that spell out their names. Assist learners in tying the leather or yarn to the key ring. Help learners arrange the beads to spell their names with a heart on either side. Encourage learners to string the beads in order on their leather or yarn, helping them to tie it off at the end so the beads stay on. **You can hang your key chain on your backpack or jacket zipper to remind you that God loves you and you love God!**

Wrapping It Up

M&P *Have available a Bible, the Witness CD (TCK), and a CD player.*

Gather all of the learners in a circle. Review the Bible story, the Big Idea, and the Faith Trait for today, using Track 7 of the CD as a review piece. Read aloud the Key Verse, 1 Kings 3:1, from your Bible. **Solomon loved the Lord.** Ask the learners to join you in prayer. **Thank you, Lord, for wisdom! Thank you for the wise friends that we have. Show us how to love and follow you every day, in all the things we do and say. Amen**

Elijah and the Widow

Session at a Glance	What You Need	What Learners Do
Ready for the Story (15 minutes)		
Welcome the Witnesses	• Witness CD (TCK), CD player	• Listen to a CD.
Story Warm-Up	• Playdough, place mats, rolling pins, cookie cutters	• Play with playdough.
Story Fire-Up	• Assorted breads, paper plates, napkins, plastic knives, butter or honey, sourdough or French bread, bowl, extra-virgin olive oil	• Taste different types of bread.
Explore the Story (20 minutes)		
Story Set-Up	• Leaflet 8 (LR), Activity Card D (TCK), Poster K (TCK), brown and tan crayons, corrugated cardboard, removable tape	• Color a picture of bread and discuss different bread ingredients.
Storytelling	• Leaflet 8 (LR), Posters H and L (TCK), Witness CD (TCK), CD player	• Hear the Bible story.
Faith Traits	• Sticker Sheet 1 (LR), magnetic tape, poster board, scissors	• Learn the Faith Trait of thankfulness.
Live the Story (25 minutes)		
Ways to Witness	• Leaflet 8 (LR), crayons	• Learn about types of bread around the world.
Kids Create	• Small plastic bottles, corks, raffia, heavy paper, scissors, paper punch, markers, extra-virgin olive oil, funnel • Bread dough, bowl, flour, place mats, rolling pins, straws, foil, permanent marker, baking sheet, oven, raffia, clear nail polish, decorative items	• Decorate olive oil bottles. • Make bread dough ornaments.
Wrapping It Up	• Witness CD (TCK), CD player	• Review the Bible story.

Bible Text

1 Kings 17:8-16

Key Verse

She went and did as Elijah said.
1 Kings 17:15

**God feeds us
in surprising ways.**

LR = Learner Resource
TCK = Teacher Class Kit
M&P = Materials and Preparation

41

Question for Reflection

What do you consider your daily bread?

Learner Goals

KNOW

God feeds people in surprising ways

GROW

in understanding that God always cares for us

SHOW

thankfulness for all of God's gifts

FACTOID

A wadi is a deep stream bed that is usually dry except during the rainy season. Some desert areas in the Middle East have many wadis.

Bible Background | What Factors Shaped This Story?

Elijah was a prophet. He prophesied against the people's unfaithfulness in turning to other gods. He also prophesied against other prophets of Yahweh who did not take justice toward the poor seriously. At the opening of 1 Kings 17, Elijah predicted a drought. Chapters 17–18 tell the story of the fulfillment of Elijah's prophecy and of Yahweh's power to end the drought, proving Yahweh's sovereignty over creation and fertility. First Kings 17:1-7 describes how God provided for Elijah as he traveled where God led him. In fulfillment of God's promise, ravens fed Elijah and he drank from a wadi until it dried up because of a drought.

What Is This Story About?

When the wadi dried up, God directed Elijah to go to Zarephath where a widow would feed him. Elijah did as God said. In fulfillment of God's word, a widow was at the gate to the town when Elijah arrived. She seems not to have received the same preparation for this encounter as had Elijah. She willingly went to bring Elijah water, but she resisted his request for bread. She had barely enough for herself and her son's last meal before they would die of starvation. Yet in response to Elijah saying, "Do not be afraid" (17:13) and speaking God's promise of provision, the widow shared what she had.

Why Is This Story Important?

The widow had to care for her son as well as herself. She had a place to live but no one on whom to rely and no wealth or income of her own. Elijah was presumptuous in asking this person—a stranger, a woman—to bring him water and bread. More, he asked this of one about to die from hunger. The prophet Elijah knew that God would provide for the widow and her son as well as himself. The woman was a person of great generosity and faith to give what little she had based on the promise of God spoken through this stranger.

Age-Level Connection

Children of all ages love bread! Because every culture has a bread of its own, help children to see that some things they may not consider to be bread *are* bread. These include tortillas, pita bread, lefse, pizza, and others. Offering samples of some of these breads of different cultures will be a good experience for this age group. Note: Before serving any food, always check with caregivers for learners who have food allergies. Provide an alternative if necessary.

What Factors Shaped This Story?

Psalms is a prayer book of hymns that express joy, sorrow, compassion, vengeance, generosity, rage, pain, fear, hope, remorse, and desire as well as many other human experiences. Psalms are also prayers of praise, thanksgiving, lament, and intercession. They tell stories of God's ways and deeds. About half of the psalms, including Psalm 23, are ascribed to King David. This tradition honors David more than it witnesses actual authorship. Psalms come from a variety of sources and voices.

What Is This Story About?

The psalm compares God to a shepherd and to a host. The shepherd provides what the sheep need, including rest, pastures for food, water, and guidance in what paths to take. Amidst the "darkest valley" (23:4)—surrounded by death—the sheep need not fear. The shepherd's protecting presence, represented by the rod and staff, is a comfort. The host provides a meal in safety amidst enemies, honors the guest with anointing, provides drink overflowing. The host provides a home for the guest's whole life. God the shepherd leads the sheep in paths of righteousness (23:3). God the host pursues the guests with goodness and mercy.

Why Is This Story Important?

This psalm is perhaps the best known of all psalms, heard frequently in hospital rooms and at funerals to comfort those familiar with the dark valley of death. This psalm's length and its message of God's constant care make it popular for memorization. The psalm uses what were in ancient times common images of daily life to convey God's care and provision. Today most people in North America are unfamiliar with sheep and shepherds. Nurse, grandmother, and hospice caregiver are possibly images today for our caring God. Though we are familiar with hosts, anointing with oil is much less common. What daily life images today convey God's hospitality and provision?

Age-Level Connection

Preschoolers and kindergartners today may not have much experience with sheep and shepherds, but they are familiar with people in their lives who watch over them and make sure they have food, clothing, and shelter, and help them to make good decisions. If the children have pets, they may begin to understand how the human owner is necessary for the pet's well-being and survival.

Teacher Prayer

Thank you, Lord, for being my shepherd! Perhaps sheep aren't the smartest creatures on earth, but sometimes I'm not either! As a shepherd in the wilderness guides his or her sheep, guide me through the rocks, crevices, and wilderness of my own life. Thank you! Amen

Question for Reflection

When you are stressed, what do you do to calm yourself and find peace?

Learner Goals

KNOW

God watches over us like a shepherd watches over his or her sheep

GROW

in security as children of God

SHOW

comfort toward others

FACTOID

Parallelism is a literary technique used often in Hebrew poetry. In parallelism, pairs of phrases or pairs of verses express the same meaning.

WITNESS WORDS

peace, comfort, safety

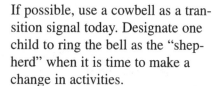

FACTOID

Rituals that confer new status may include anointing, putting oil on the person, as in anointing kings or priests. People may also be anointed at death.

▶ Transition Tip ◀

If possible, use a cowbell as a transition signal today. Designate one child to ring the bell as the "shepherd" when it is time to make a change in activities.

Ready for the Story (15 minutes)

Welcome the Witnesses

M&P *Play the Witness CD from the Age 2–Grade 4 Teacher Class Kit (TCK) as the learners arrive.*

Welcome all of the children, especially any who may have been sick or gone the last time. If you have any guests, be sure to welcome them, introducing yourself and the learners. **Welcome back to Sunday school! I'm so glad each one of you is here!**

Story Warm-Up

M&P *Display Posters M and Q (TCK) where you will tell the Bible story and where everyone can see them. Set out stuffed animals or plastic animals.*

After you have greeted the learners, invite them to play with the animals. Talk with learners while they are playing. **Do any of you live on a farm? Have any of you ever been to a farm?** We cannot assume that most children have knowledge of farm and farm animal life today. Many children, however, may have been to a petting zoo or fair, and can relate to that experience. After a few more minutes of play, ask the learners to put the animals back where they found them. If they have not noticed the posters, point them out to the learners. Point to Poster M. **What does the picture in this poster make you think of?** Point to Poster Q. **What is the person in this poster doing?**

Story Fire-Up

M&P *Hide a stuffed sheep somewhere in the class when the children are busy playing with the animals or cleaning up. You will need a small bell such as a jingle bell. Continue to display Poster Q (TCK).*

Gather together in a circle and talk about the sheep and shepherd on the poster. **What does a shepherd do for the sheep? How does a shepherd or other caretaker take care of animals? What does a farmer do to make sure his or her animals are taken care of?** After the learners have shared some of their thoughts, share with them that there is a sheep hiding somewhere in this room! **Sometimes a shepherd has to find sheep that are lost! As you look for the sheep, I will "baa" softly if you are far away from it and "baa" louder the closer you get to it. When you get close enough and I ring this bell** (*ring the bell*) **quickly sit down right where you are. Then you can join me in "baaing" until everyone has found the lost sheep!** After everyone has found the sheep and is sitting down, play the game again, depending on time. Otherwise, you will be in a sitting position ready for the story.

Explore the Story <small>(20 minutes)</small>

Story Set-Up

M&P *Gather Leaflet 11 from the Pre-Kindergarten/Kindergarten Learner Resource (LR) and crayons or markers. Display Poster K (TCK) and have the Session 11 Big Idea sentence strip from Activity Card D (TCK) and removable tape available. Remove the Session 10 sentence strip from the poster and display it somewhere in the classroom.*

Ask a learner to help you hand out the leaflets. Look together at the pastoral scene on the front, and explain the color code to the learners. As the learners color the scene, talk about peaceful places. **Are there places like the one in the picture that you like to go to? Are there other peaceful places in our town that you've seen?** When the learners have finished, review the Big Ideas that have been presented so far, using the sentence strips you have displayed in the classroom. Read the Session 11 Big Idea, found on the back of the leaflet, aloud. **God provides comfort and safety.** Invite a learner to tape the Big Idea sentence strip to the space on the poster. **How does God help you feel safe?**

Storytelling

M&P *Make sure each learner has Leaflet 11 (LR). You will need the Witness CD (TCK), a CD player, and a Bible. Make sure Poster Q (TCK) is displayed.*

Play Track 11 on the CD as the learners settle in to hear the story. After they are settled, lay your Bible in your lap and open it to Psalms. Read the Bible story inside the leaflet, then read it from your Bible. **Have you heard this psalm before?** Point out the poster. **Does this poster make you feel peaceful? How is it comforting? Would this be a place where sheep would like to be? Many people in Bible times had sheep, were shepherds, or knew someone who was a shepherd. People in the Bible knew that God was like a shepherd because God takes good care of people like a shepherd takes good care of the sheep.**

FAITH Traits

M&P *You will need the Session 11 Faith Trait sticker on Sticker Sheet 1 (LR), magnetic tape, each learner's poster board, and scissors.*

Review the Faith Trait words you have studied so far this semester, helping the learners repeat the words aloud together. **Today's Faith Trait is peace. Having peace means being calm and not afraid. How does God help us to feel peace? How is there peace in the world? How can we share the peace of God with others?** Have the learners attach the Faith Trait sticker to the poster board next to the space where they cut out their last piece. Help them cut the poster board around the shape of the sticker and attach a piece of magnetic tape to the back. Encourage learners to add this piece to their puzzle at home. Read aloud the Big Idea for this session again. **God provides comfort and safety. Has there been a time in your life when God has comforted you?** *(Answers might include in a thunderstorm, when they were riding the school bus for the first time, or when they were in the park and a big dog was barking at them.)* **No matter what the situation, God will always be there for you.**

Kid Connect

Talk with the children about pets or animals you may have had, either as a child or now. What kinds of things did/do you do to take care of them? If the children have pets, ask what they do to care for the pets in their lives. Remind them that animals in their care depend on them for everything.

More Movement

Act out Psalm 23 with the children, starting with you as the shepherd, guiding the children (the sheep). Invite others to take turns being the shepherd, but do not force anyone to do so. As you do this, play Track 11 of the Witness CD (TCK) or read the version in the leaflet.

Teacher Boost

You are like a shepherd to the children you teach, not only during class time, but whenever you see them in the congregation or community. Never underestimate the important impact you have on their lives, even though it may seem insignificant at times. You are doing God's work with these young children!

Witnesses in the World

Is there an animal shelter in your community? Perhaps you and your learners could sponsor a pet food drive in your congregation to provide food for the shelter.

GREAT good byes

As learners are leaving, talk to each one. **God is like our good shepherd, always with us to take care of us and to comfort us.**

Live the Story (25 minutes)

Ways to Witness

M&P *Each learner will need Leaflet 11 (LR) and crayons or markers. Listen to Track 11 of the Witness CD (TCK).*

Ask the learners to look at the next page in the leaflet and look at the pictures of different ways to honor God. Review and talk about the things David did to love and honor God. **In what ways can we love and honor God? Circle the pictures that show how you honor God.** Invite the children to share their ideas. Play Track 11 of the CD as a way to help the learners become familiar with this psalm.

Kids Create (Choose One!)

M&P *Stuffed Sheep Mobiles: Draw an outline of a sheep on 9" x 12" (23 cm x 30 cm) white construction paper. Hold two pieces of white paper together and cut out the pattern, making a set for each learner. You will also need tissue paper or foam packing material, a paper punch, black yarn, and tape. Hold each pair of sheep together and punch holes evenly around the edges for lacing. Clip them together.*

Peace Crayon Wash: Each learner will need one 9" x 12" (23 cm x 30 cm) sheet of white construction paper. Write "Peace" in block letters in white crayon on each sheet. You will also need watercolor paints, small containers of water, paintbrushes, and paint shirts. Make a sample crayon wash and partially complete it to show the learners.

Stuffed Sheep Mobiles: Give each learner a pair of sheep shapes and a long length of yarn (put tape around one end to make lacing easier). Help learners tie one end of the black yarn through a pair of holes at one point of the sheep to begin lacing, then show the learners how to lace their sheep pieces together. Help with lacing if necessary. Leave a portion open to insert small pieces of crumpled tissue paper or foam packing material, then finish the lacing. Help tie off the yarn. Attach black yarn to the top for hanging. **These sheep remind us that God is like our shepherd and we are like God's sheep!**

Peace Crayon Wash: Show the learners your partially completed crayon wash. Hand out the construction paper you've prepared. Invite learners to choose one or more colors to wash over their pictures. Imagine their surprise when they see the word you wrote! Set the paintings aside to dry. **These pictures can help make us feel peaceful like Psalm 23 does!**

Wrapping It Up

M&P *Have the Witness CD (TCK) and a CD player available.*

Gather together to close the session. Talk about the Big Idea. **God is so important to us in our lives, just like a shepherd is important to his or her sheep.** Play Track 11 of the CD, reviewing Psalm 23 together. Remind the learners that there are fun things for them to do at home in their leaflets. Have the learners sit in a circle and hold the hands of the learners sitting next to them as you pray. **Dear Lord, thank you for sheep and shepherds! Thank you for good friends and for the chance to learn to know and love you more. Amen**

Jonah and the Whale

12

Session at a Glance	What You Need	What Learners Do
Ready for the Story (15 minutes)		
Welcome the Witnesses	• Witness CD (TCK), CD player	• Listen to a CD.
Story Warm-Up	• Water table or large dishpans, water, plastic tarp or tablecloth, toy boats and sea creatures, towels	• Engage in water play.
Story Fire-Up	• Reproducible Sheet B (TCK), colored paper, fish crackers, plastic cups, water, napkins	• Have a snack and make an origami whale.
Explore the Story (20 minutes)		
Story Set-Up	• Leaflet 12 (LR), Sticker Sheet 2 (LR), Activity Card D (TCK), Poster K (TCK), removable tape, crayons or markers	• Connect the dots to make a picture.
Storytelling	• Leaflet 12 (LR), Reproducible Sheet A (TCK), scissors, tape, crayons	• Learn and retell the story of Jonah and the big fish.
Faith Traits	• Sticker Sheet 1 (LR), magnetic tape, poster board, scissors	• Learn about the Faith Trait of obedience.
Live the Story (25 minutes)		
Ways to Witness	• Leaflet 12 (LR), crayons or markers	• Think about and draw a picture of a favorite safe place.
Kids Create	• Water bottles with lids, permanent marker, water, cooking oil, blue food coloring, funnel, small boats or fish, strapping tape • Mural paper, yellow and green washable paint, paint shirts, paintbrush, hand wipes or water and paper towels	• Make wave bottles. • Make sunflower pictures.
Wrapping It Up	• Activity Card A (TCK), Witness CD (TCK), CD player	• Review the Bible story.

Bible Text

Jonah 1–4

Key Verse

You are a gracious God and merciful, slow to anger, and abounding in steadfast love. Jonah 4:2

God always knows where we are.

LR = Learner Resource
TCK = Teacher Class Kit
M&P = Materials and Preparation

Teacher Prayer

Dear Lord, sometimes I feel like Jonah, swallowed up in life! Help me to take time each day to stop and listen to you, to ask for your help when I am unsure, and to enjoy the humorous things you bring to my days! Amen

Question for Reflection

Have you ever run away from God or from something God wanted you to do?

Learner Goals

KNOW

God always knows where we are

GROW

in understanding that God is gracious and merciful

SHOW

others how to follow rules

FACTOID

Nineveh was located in ancient Mesopotamia, modern-day Iraq. Nineveh was the capital of Assyria, which at one time conquered part of ancient Israel.

Bible Background | **What Factors Shaped This Story?**

God's ways are not our ways. God's justice is not our justice. We might consider it unfair that people who have been wicked should receive God's mercy. Even if people turn "from their evil ways" (3:10), we may think that somehow people should have to pay for their sins. That is not God's way. The book of Jonah is a humorous and serious tale about this problem for our thinking about justice. The story also helps us to reflect on our own sense of righteousness and our need for God's mercy. Jonah's reluctance as a prophet can be compared and contrasted to other prophets who were also reluctant, such as Moses (Exodus 3:10—4:17).

What Is This Story About?

God called Jonah to preach repentance to the wicked Ninevites, but Jonah tried to escape that call. By turning his back on God, Jonah endangered the sailors on whose ship he tried to escape—as if there were a place to which Jonah could go to escape God's presence. In spite of Jonah, the sailors came to worship God. After they threw Jonah off the ship, a great fish swallowed him. The fish probably saved Jonah's life, but the fish's belly must have seemed like a prison to him. Jonah repented. Again God called Jonah to preach repentance to the Ninevites. He went in spite of himself. The Ninevites, who had forty days, repented in one! Jonah was miserable.

Why Is This Story Important?

We are called from our ways and our sensibilities to God's ways. We are called to share the news of God's love and new life in Jesus Christ and to call others to repentance. Sometimes we would rather see vengeance on our enemies than see them receive God's mercy. Sometimes we would prefer to be separate from those we do not like rather than be reconciled with them. We can try all sorts of things to escape God's call. God not only does not give up on our enemies, God does not give up on us!

Age-Level Connection

Most young children are familiar with the story of Jonah and the whale, or the big fish. Whales, the ark, dinosaurs—anything of immense size is fascinating to them! Try to keep the focus on the true meaning of this story, that God always knows where we are and is watching out for us.

Ready for the Story (15 minutes)

Welcome the Witnesses

M&P *Play the Witness CD from the Age 2–Grade 4 Teacher Class Kit (TCK) as the learners arrive.*

Welcome the learners to class, especially any who may have been gone last week. **Hi, everybody! How was your week?**

Story Warm-Up

M&P *Set up a water table with several inches (centimeters) of water in the bottom or use large dishpans. Put a plastic tarp or tablecloth under the table to help with spills. Add small plastic boats and sea creatures to the water. Provide plenty of towels.*

Invite learners into the area where the water table is and encourage them to play with the water, boats, and sea creatures. Explain that they should be careful when walking around the area because the floor might be slippery. When they have had time to play and explore, have everyone help with cleanup and dry their hands.

Story Fire-Up

M&P *You will need fish crackers, plastic cups, napkins, and water. Note: Before serving any food, always check with caregivers for learners who have food allergies. Provide an alternative if necessary. Make an origami whale using the directions on Reproducible Sheet B (TCK) to see whether it is appropriate to use with your learners. If it is, provide sheets of colored paper, one per learner.*

Gather the learners around a table and offer them glasses of water and the fish crackers. As you are snacking, talk about the Bible story for today. **Today's story is about a man named Jonah and a whale or a big fish. Has anyone heard this story before? Today we will learn more about Jonah, and that even though he ran away from God, God was always with him.** If the origami whale is not too difficult for the learners, give each of them a square of paper. Show learners how to make the whale, using the instructions on the reproducible sheet, pausing after each step so learners can copy what you do. Offer help to learners who may be having difficulties. Be sure each learner puts his or her name on the whale so they don't get mixed up when it's time to go home.

Witness WORDS

obey, gracious, steadfast

FACTOID

Fasting and wearing sackcloth were signs of repentance. Other signs were sitting in ashes or rubbing them on one's face or body, weeping, and tearing one's garments.

 Transition Tip

Use a clapping pattern as your transition signal today. Have the learners listen while you clap, then copy the clapping pattern after you. Try this several times. Children enjoy it and it is a good break in the routine.

Kid Connect

Children and adults alike have often felt like Jonah: asked to do something they really don't want to do. Help learners understand and connect even more by relating experiences in their lives to this story. For example, many children have had experience with not wanting to complete a household chore such as cleaning their rooms or setting the table. How might these kinds of things help the learners relate to the way that Jonah felt?

More Movement

The Bible tells us that Jonah ran away from God. Act out the story of Jonah running away from God by having the learners run in place, then pretend to climb aboard a ship. Next, have the learners sway as the ship rocks back and forth, going faster and faster as the storm gets worse. Finally, have them sit down with crossed legs and their arms over their heads, swaying inside the whale.

Explore the Story (20 minutes)

Story Set-Up

M&P *Gather Leaflet 12 from the Pre-Kindergarten/Kindergarten Learner Resource (LR) and have the Jonah sticker from Sticker Sheet 2 (LR) and crayons or markers available. Display Poster K (TCK) and have the Session 12 Big Idea sentence strip from Activity Card D (TCK) and removable tape available. Remove the Session 11 sentence strip from the poster and display it somewhere in the classroom.*

Ask a learner to help you hand out the leaflets. Show them the dot-to-dot activity on the front of the leaflet and read aloud the directions for this activity. Encourage learners to complete the dot-to-dot picture, then add the sticker of Jonah inside the whale. Review the Big Ideas that have been presented so far, using the sentence strips you have displayed in the classroom. Introduce this session's Big Idea, found on the back of the leaflet. **God always knows where we are, and God knew where Jonah was too!** Invite a learner to tape the Big Idea sentence strip to the space on the poster.

Storytelling

M&P *Make sure each learner has Leaflet 12 (LR). Copy Reproducible Sheet A (TCK) for each child and cut the cube pattern out so each learner can recreate the story. Have tape and crayons or markers available.*

Have the learners open their leaflets and look at the Bible story pictures. Read aloud the Bible story of Jonah and the whale. **Jonah ran away from God, but God still found him. No matter where we are, God is with us!** Give each learner a cube pattern you cut out. Review six story events. Have the learners illustrate the story events in no particular order on the cube. Assist learners with folding and taping the cube together. To retell the story, have a learner roll his or her cube and tell about the part of the story that is on top.

FAITH Traits

M&P *You will need the Session 12 Faith Trait sticker on Sticker Sheet 1 (LR), magnetic tape, each learner's poster board, and scissors.*

Review the Faith Traits you have learned so far. **The Faith Trait for today is obedience. To obey means to follow the rules. When we obey, God is pleased.** Have the learners attach the Faith Trait sticker to the poster board next to the space where they cut out their last piece. Help them cut the poster board around the shape of the sticker and attach a strip of magnetic tape to the back. Encourage learners to add this piece to their puzzle at home.

Live the Story (25 minutes)

Ways to Witness

M&P *Each learner will need Leaflet 12 (LR) and crayons or markers.*

Ask the learners to look at the next leaflet page. Read the activity aloud to them. **Do you have a favorite place you go where you can be safe? Do you have a tree house or playhouse where you can go to get away?** Encourage learners to draw a picture of their favorite safe place on the page. Walk around as the learners are drawing and comment positively about their pictures, such as, "What a great place! I wish I had a place like that."

Kids Create (Choose One!)

M&P *Wave Bottles: Each learner will need a clean, empty water bottle with a lid. You will also need a permanent marker, blue food coloring, water, cooking oil, a funnel, small plastic boats or fish that will fit into the opening of the bottle, and clear strapping tape.*

Sunflower Prints: You will need mural paper, yellow and green washable paint, a wide paintbrush (like one used for house painting), paint shirts, and hand wipes or water and paper towels.

Wave Bottles: Give each learner a bottle and write her or his name on it with a permanent marker. Have learners help you to use a funnel to fill the bottles two-thirds full with water. Encourage learners to add a few drops of blue food coloring and a few drops of cooking oil. Then they can add a small boat or fish and close the bottles tightly. Check to make sure the caps are tight, and seal them securely with strapping tape. **You can make waves by turning your bottle on its side to gently rock it back and forth. How would the waves have looked when Jonah was on the boat in the storm?**

Sunflower Prints: Write each child's name on a large sheet of mural paper. Have each learner use the paintbrush to paint a large stem with green paint in the center of the paper. Then paint the learner's hands with yellow paint and show how to press his or her open handprints around the top of the stem to make a sunflower. After everyone has painted her or his flowers, repaint their hands with green paint and show how to hold their fingers together to make a green leaf on either side of the stem. Have the learners clean their hands. **Jonah loved the plant that God grew near him!**

Wrapping It Up

M&P *Have the Witness CD (TCK), Activity Card A (TCK), and a CD player available.*

Gather together for the session closing. Review the Big Idea and play Track 12 of the CD as a story review. Lay the activity card pieces on the table. **Who can help put this story puzzle together in the right order?** Remind the learners about the Faith Trait for today. **How can we obey God, our parents, and other people in our lives?** Remind the learners to share their leaflets and the leaflet activities with their families at home. Close with a prayer, asking that God watch over each child in a special way this week.

Teacher Boost

How do you feel about the way the sessions are going? Are the children responding to the message of God's love and care for them? If you could change something in your time with the children, what would it be? It is possible to do this in your setting?

Witnesses in the World

Is your church participating in a mission project in another part of the world? If so, how can you and your class help? Could you spearhead a project in which the entire Sunday school would be willing to participate?

GREAT good byes

Hug the learners or give them a special pat on the shoulder as they leave, and remind them to watch for the ways that God cares for them in the coming week.

Mary Visits Elizabeth

Bible Text

Luke 1:39-56

Key Verse

My soul magnifies the Lord.
Luke 1:46

God brings joy.

Session at a Glance	What You Need	What Learners Do
Ready for the Story (15 minutes)		
Welcome the Witnesses	• Witness CD (TCK), CD player	• Listen to a CD.
Story Warm-Up	• Magnifying glasses, variety of nature objects	• Examine objects through a magnifying glass.
Story Fire-Up	• Sheets of craft foam, permanent markers, paint shirts, stapler	• Make "Child of God" armbands.
Explore the Story (20 minutes)		
Story Set-Up	• Leaflet 13 (LR), Sticker Sheet 2 (LR), Activity Card D (TCK), Posters K and S (TCK), removable tape	• Finish a picture.
Storytelling	• Leaflet 13 (LR)	• Learn the Bible story.
Faith Traits	• Sticker Sheet 1 (LR), magnetic tape, poster board, scissors	• Learn about the Faith Trait of joy.
Live the Story (25 minutes)		
Ways to Witness	• Leaflet 13 (LR), crayons or markers	• Learn about and share different places where they praise God.
Kids Create	• Clamp clothespins, permanent marker, cord, scissors • Fleece material, scissors	• Make name necklaces. • Make blankets.
Wrapping It Up	• Poster S (TCK), Witness CD (TCK), CD player	• Review the Bible story.

LR = Learner Resource
TCK = Teacher Class Kit
M&P = Materials and Preparation

Bible Background — What Factors Shaped This Story?

Mary, Jesus' mother, and Elizabeth, John the Baptist's mother, were relatives. Each became pregnant in seemingly impossible ways: Elizabeth first, then six months later Mary (1:26). Elizabeth was past childbearing age and thought to be barren. Mary was a virgin and her pregnancy resulted from the Holy Spirit, not sexual relations with Joseph, to whom she was engaged. What seemed impossible was possible with God. From the same messenger who told her of her pregnancy, Mary learned that Elizabeth had also conceived a child. Mary lived in the town of Nazareth in Galilee. Elizabeth lived in the hills of Judea.

What Is This Story About?

Mary went—apparently on her own—to be with Elizabeth. Upon Mary's arrival, Elizabeth knew that Mary had conceived the one who would be called Son of God. Mary's song (verses 46-55) is called the Magnificat, after the first word of the song in Latin. It reveals Mary's joy at God's blessing and tells of God's justice and mercy. God's mercy turns the world upside down: the powerful brought down, the lowly lifted up, the hungry filled, the rich empty. As a testament to this message's importance, every day somewhere in the church Christians sing Mary's song as part of the evening liturgy known as vespers.

Why Is This Story Important?

Nazareth in Galilee and the hill country of Judea were not what we would call important places. In that world women did not have the status they have today in much of the world. Yet in that time and place, through two women, God announced and set in motion God's coming among us in flesh. They were not noble women, but lowly. Their pregnancies were likewise surprising. The prophecy of God's reign as heard in Mary's song was already being realized in God's choice of these women and the communities of which they were a part.

Age-Level Connection

Young children—as well as adults—have trouble understanding the mystery and awe that surround the stories of Mary and Elizabeth and the births of their children. God's love and purpose is something we can't explain, yet we can help children know that God's plans are always for good, and that sometimes things that seem impossible are not.

Teacher Prayer

Dear Lord, thank you for the joy of good news! Thank you for the babies and children who bless our lives and bring us joy. Amen

Question for Reflection

How do you share joy with the people in your life?

Learner Goals

KNOW

God planned for Jesus to be our Savior

GROW

in understanding that God uses ordinary people to do extraordinary things

SHOW

joy in their lives as children of God

FACTOID

At the time of Jesus' birth, Judea was the area surrounding Jerusalem with Idumea to the south and Samaria and Galilee to the north.

WITNESS WORDS

joy, blessed, magnifies

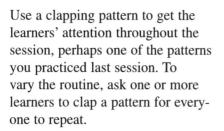

FACTOID

Mary's song echoes that of Hannah's song in 1 Samuel 2:1-10, celebrating God's answer to her prayer. Hannah, who was childless, prayed for a son.

▶ **Transition Tip** ◀

Use a clapping pattern to get the learners' attention throughout the session, perhaps one of the patterns you practiced last session. To vary the routine, ask one or more learners to clap a pattern for everyone to repeat.

Ready for the Story (15 minutes)

Welcome the Witnesses

M&P *Play the Witness CD from the Age 2–Grade 4 Teacher Class Kit (TCK) as the learners arrive.*

Welcome all as they arrive for class, making a special point to thank the parents or caregivers for bringing their children. **Welcome back to Sunday school! I'm excited to see all of you today!**

Story Warm-Up

M&P *Set several magnifying glasses on a table, along with objects from nature such as feathers, leaves, snakeskin, rocks, or other interesting items.*

As the learners gather, show them the magnifying glasses and items you have collected. Encourage them to take turns looking at the items through the magnifying glasses. **When we look through this glass, it magnifies—or makes larger—the things we are looking at. Details of these items can be seen better when we look through a magnifying glass. To** *magnify* **means to make larger. Today's Bible verse is "My soul magnifies the Lord." Mary said this when she was praising God as much as she could.** After everyone has had a chance to examine some of the items, set the items and the magnifying glasses aside. If there is time later, some learners may want to return to this area and look at these objects again.

Story Fire-Up

M&P *Cut strips of craft foam 3" (8 cm) wide and long enough to go around the upper part of each learner's arm as an armband. Write "(Child's name) is a child of God" on each armband with a permanent marker. You will need a stapler, permanent markers, and paint shirts.*

We are all children of God! God has made the world and all that is in it, and that includes us. Let's make "Children of God" armbands to wear as a reminder. Have the learners put on paint shirts. Distribute the foam pieces to the learners. Encourage them to decorate the armbands around the text, but caution the learners to be careful because the markers are permanent and will stain their hands and clothes. As they finish decorating, help fasten each armband by stapling the ends together. **I'm glad to see you, *(child's name)*, child of God!**

Explore the Story (20 minutes)

Story Set-Up

M&P *Gather Leaflet 13 from the Pre-Kindergarten/Kindergarten Learner Resource (LR) and have the Mary and Elizabeth sticker from Sticker Sheet 2 (LR) available. Display Posters K and S (TCK) and have the Session 13 Big Idea sentence strip from Activity Card D (TCK) and removable tape available. Remove the Session 12 sentence strip from the poster and display it somewhere in the classroom.*

Ask one of the learners to help hand out the leaflets. Look at the front and read the sentences about Mary aloud. Encourage the learners to complete the picture by adding the sticker of Mary and Elizabeth. Review the Big Ideas that have been presented so far, using the sentence strips you have displayed in the classroom. Introduce the Big Idea, found on the back of the leaflet. **God brings joy.** Invite a learner to tape the Big Idea sentence strip to the space on the poster. **Can you name some of the things in your life that make you happy?** Point out Poster S that shows joy and talk about it as well.

Storytelling

M&P *Make sure each learner has Leaflet 13 (LR).*

Ask the learners to open their leaflets and find the Bible story about Mary and Elizabeth. Read the story to the learners. **Do you have babies at your house? Do you know any babies? Babies are so much fun! They keep us busy, but they remind us of how much God loves us. Mary and Elizabeth were so happy that God was with them, and that God loved them and their babies, even before the babies were born. Their babies were children of God, just as you are children of God!**

FAITH Traits

M&P *You will need the Session 13 Faith Trait sticker on Sticker Sheet 1 (LR), magnetic tape, each learner's poster board, and scissors.*

Review all of the Faith Traits you have learned with the children so far. **Today's Faith Trait is joy. When you are joyful, you are really happy. How do you know when someone is feeling joyful?** Have the learners attach the Faith Trait sticker to the poster board next to the space where they cut out their last piece. Help them cut the poster board around the shape of the sticker and attach a strip of magnetic tape to the back. Encourage learners to add this piece to their puzzle at home. Review the Big Idea for this session. **God brings joy. How does God bring joy to your life?** Share some examples of the joy God brings to your life and encourage the learners to share examples too.

Kid Connect

Young children can change moods at the drop of a hat! Sometimes we wish we could forget things that bother us as easily as children do and just focus on praising God. Encourage the learners to share the things for which they love to thank and praise God, perhaps making a list of these things on chart paper and posting it as a "praise wall."

More Movement

Use this simple rhyme and these actions as a praise movement activity to God.

Thank you, God! (*Step forward and raise hands high.*)

Thank you, God! (*Step back and raise hands high.*)

For all of the world, (*Hold arms out to sides and spin around to the right.*)

For everything in my life, (*Hold arms out to sides and spin around to the left.*)

Thank you, God! (*Kneel, raise hands above head, and look up.*)

Teacher Boost

God does use ordinary people to do extraordinary things! Remember this when you don't feel you are reaching the children in your class the way you hoped you would.

Witnesses in the World

If your congregation has a child-care center or infant care facility, find out how you and your class could help. Perhaps donations would be helpful, such as disposable diapers and wipes. Or maybe you and the learners could paint a wall mural that the younger children would enjoy. Four-, five-, and six-year-olds love to offer their help, especially to those younger than they are.

Go Global!

Check out the Session 13 Go Global! activity on Reproducible Sheets I and J (TCK). See page 3 of this guide.

GREAT good byes

As the children leave, remind them with a smile that you love to be with them and that you look forward to seeing them next week. Call each by name, referring to their name necklaces and "Child of God" armbands. Tell each of them to have a joyful week.

Live the Story (25 minutes)

Ways to Witness

M&P *Each learner will need Leaflet 13 (LR) and crayons or markers.*

Ask the learners to look at the next page of the leaflet. **You can praise God! I can praise God! Everyone can praise God! We can praise God at church, but we can praise God other places too. Where do you like to praise God?** After the children have shared their ideas, explain that the learners should look at the photos of places where they can praise God. **Circle the places where you can praise God.**

Kids Create (Choose One!)

M&P *Clothespin Name Necklaces: You will need one clamp clothespin for each letter in each learner's first name. With the clamp end of the clothespin at the top, print one letter on each clothespin with a permanent marker. Cut a 24" (61 cm) length of cord for each child.*

Fleece Blankets: You will need two approximately 30" x 32" (76 cm x 81 cm) pieces of fleece for each learner. Invite adult volunteers to help.

Clothespin Name Necklaces: Give each learner a length of cord and the letter clothespins they will need to make their name. Have them lay the clothespins on the table in the correct order, then demonstrate how to clip the clothespins to the cord to spell their names. Offer as much help as needed. When they are done clipping the clothespin letters to the cord, tie the ends together to complete the necklace. **God knows every child's name because each child is special to God!**

Fleece Blankets: Give each child two pieces of fleece, place them back-to-back, and cut a fringe in each side. The fringe should be at least 4" (10 cm) long. Demonstrate how to knot the matching pieces of fringe from each piece of fleece together to finish the blanket edge. Talk with the learners as they are working on this fine-motor activity of tying. Have adult volunteers help learners tie the fringes. **Babies like to have a special blanket to help them go to sleep. Will Elizabeth and Mary's babies need special blankets? Sometimes people of all ages like to have a soft blanket to help them sleep. This could be a special blanket for you, or you could share it with a friend.**

Wrapping It Up

M&P *Display Poster S (TCK) and have the Witness CD (TCK) and a CD player available.*

Ask the learners to join you in a circle for your closing time together. Play Track 13 of the CD, and review the Big Idea. **Joy is also the Faith Trait for today.** Point out the poster and review some of the things learners shared that bring them joy. Ask everyone to hold hands and join in a prayer to thank and praise God for the good things in their lives. Start the prayer, and then allow time for the learners to contribute. **Dear God, thank you always for… We praise you, God! Amen.** Remind the learners to use their leaflets at home with their families.

John Is Born

Session at a Glance	What You Need	What Learners Do
Ready for the Story (15 minutes)		
Welcome the Witnesses	• CD of lullabies, CD player	• Listen to a CD.
Story Warm-Up	• Picture books of babies and young children, dolls, doll items	• Play in the home center.
Story Fire-Up	• Crepe paper streamers, scissors	• Shake streamers for joy.
Explore the Story (20 minutes)		
Story Set-Up	• Leaflet 14 (LR), Activity Card D (TCK), Poster K (TCK), removable tape, crayons or markers	• Find pictures of things babies need.
Storytelling	• Leaflet 14 (LR), streamers from "Story Fire-Up"	• Learn the Bible story.
Faith Traits	• Sticker Sheet 1 (LR), magnetic tape, poster board, scissors	• Learn about the Faith Trait of thankfulness.
Live the Story (25 minutes)		
Ways to Witness	• Leaflet 14 (LR), crayons or markers	• Show thankfulness for their families.
Kids Create	• Construction paper, streamers from "Story Fire-Up," paper punch, stapler, tape, yarn, colorful paper scraps, glue, scissors • Reproducible Sheet G (TCK), Sticker Sheet 1 (LR), heavy paper, scissors	• Make wind socks. • Make Advent calendars.
Wrapping It Up	• Witness CD (TCK), CD player	• Review the Bible story.

Bible Text

Luke 1:57-80

Key Verse

He has raised up a mighty savior for us. Luke 1:69

BIG Idea

Speak the news— celebrate God's gifts!

LR = Learner Resource
TCK = Teacher Class Kit
M&P = Materials and Preparation

71

Teacher Prayer

Dear Lord, am I as impatient as these children are sometimes? Now that Christmas is so near, their energy level keeps going up while mine seems to be going down! Help me to capture some of their joy and excitement at this season as I try to keep my focus on you during this busy time of the year. Amen

Question for Reflection

How are you preparing your heart for the coming Christ child?

Learner Goals

KNOW

about John the Baptist

GROW

in knowing God's plan of salvation

SHOW

praise to God

FACTOID

Circumcision is a sign of God's covenant with Abraham (Genesis 17:11). Christians, Muslims, and Jews regard Abraham as their ancestor and commonly practice circumcision.

Bible Background | **What Factors Shaped This Story?**

Elizabeth was barren and past childbearing age when she conceived John. In the Jerusalem temple God's messenger had announced to Elizabeth's spouse, Zechariah, that she would bear a son. Because of his unbelief, Zechariah was made mute. When he came out of the temple waving his hands and unable to speak, the people who saw him knew he had seen a vision. Elizabeth remained in seclusion, not only because this was the common practice for pregnant women but perhaps also because her pregnancy was so unusual. Her relative, Mary, who became pregnant six months after Elizabeth did, came to stay with her for about three months during their pregnancies.

What Is This Story About?

The birth was great cause for celebration. Only God could have done this! Elizabeth and Zechariah took the child to be circumcised and, the community expected, to be named after his father. Elizabeth stated that his name was to be John. The angel Gabriel commanded this in Luke 1:13. Normally Elizabeth's protests would have been ignored, but Zechariah affirmed her and his voice was restored. Joyful as the neighbors were, these events threw them off. Who or what would the child born under these circumstances become? Zechariah's song, called the Benedictus after the first word in Latin, celebrates God's grace, God's promises fulfilled, and the prophetic role the child John would play in the unfolding of God's plan.

Why Is This Story Important?

God was doing amazing things! Not only the conception and birth itself, not only Zechariah becoming mute and regaining his voice, but other details of the story point to God's ways. How unusual that a woman—the mother—named the child! Perhaps the most powerful witness to God's ways was the people's reaction to all these happenings. The people were both joyful and afraid. Wonderful events can be

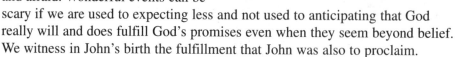

scary if we are used to expecting less and not used to anticipating that God really will and does fulfill God's promises even when they seem beyond belief. We witness in John's birth the fulfillment that John was also to proclaim.

Age-Level Connection

Young children can understand what it means to be thankful, and they have many reasons in their lives to be thankful. While it is easy for both children and adults to show gratitude and thankfulness for material things in our lives, it is often harder to learn to be thankful for and identify nonmaterial things.

Ready for the Story (15 minutes)

Welcome the Witnesses

M&P *You will need a CD of lullabies and a CD player. Play the music as the children arrive.*

Welcome all of the learners and parents or caregivers and extend a special welcome to anyone who has been sick or gone for a time. **Hello! We're going to have some fun today! We are going to learn about a special baby who was born before Jesus.**

Story Warm-Up

M&P *Set out picture books of babies and young children. Include baby dolls and doll items such as clothes, bottle, rattles, and other baby toys in the home center area.*

Encourage the learners to play in the home center, dressing and playing with the dolls and other home center items. Show them the picture books of babies and young children. **Do you have scrapbooks or baby books at home? Isn't it amazing that we all were babies once?**

Story Fire-Up

M&P *You will need crepe paper streamers in several colors. Cut them in 12" (30 cm) lengths.*

Give each learner several streamers to hold. **You can wave your streamers to show your joy while I read the Bible story. Let's practice joyfully waving the streamers together!**

WORDS

celebrate, thankfulness, praise

FACTOID

The Holy Spirit is important throughout Luke and Acts, beginning with John's birth foretold (Luke 1) and the church's birth at Pentecost (Acts 2).

 Transition Tip

A set of wind chimes or a bell can make a quiet transition signal, especially as children become more excited the closer it gets to Christmas. A bell is quiet and slows everyone down, but is not a jarring sound.

Kid Connect

Young children don't need to focus on the conception of John or Jesus, but on the miracle of babies. Although some children in the group may be the baby of their family themselves, they may know of cousins or neighbors who have babies.

More Movement

Play joyful music, either on the Witness CD (TCK) or another praise CD, and let the children joyfully dance to the music!

Explore the Story (20 minutes)

Story Set-Up

M&P *Gather Leaflet 14 from the Pre-Kindergarten/Kindergarten Learner Resource and have crayons or markers available. Display Poster K from the Age 2–Grade 4 Teacher Class Kit (TCK) and have the Session 14 Big Idea sentence strip from Activity Card D (TCK) and removable tape available. Remove the Session 13 sentence strip from the poster and display it somewhere in the classroom.*

Ask one of the learners to hand out the leaflets, and invite everyone to look at the front. **When babies are born, they need lots of love and care. Babies need other things too. What things do babies need? Draw a circle around items that they need.** Review the Big Ideas that have been presented so far, using the sentence strips you have displayed in the classroom. Read the Big Idea, found on the back of the leaflet. **Speak the news—celebrate God's gifts!** Invite a learner to tape the Big Idea sentence strip to the space on the poster. **At this time of year, we often think about gifts. But instead of thinking about the gifts we would like to get or give to others, we should think about the gifts God has given us. What gifts that God has given us can we share with others?** Let the learners share some of the gifts that they can share with others. **Wow! God has given us so many gifts to be thankful for!**

Storytelling

M&P *Make sure each learner has Leaflet 14 (LR) and their streamers from "Story Fire-Up."*

Ask learners to turn to the next page in their leaflets, to the story about the birth of John the Baptist. **While I read, wave your streamers every time there is something happy in the story.** Read the story aloud. If necessary, wave your streamers when you'd like the children to wave theirs. **Why were people surprised when Elizabeth said the baby's name would be John? Do any of you have the same name as your mother or father or anyone else in your family? John the Baptist was the cousin of Jesus, and he loved God just like Jesus did.**

FAITH Traits

M&P *You will need the Session 14 Faith Trait sticker on Sticker Sheet 1 (LR), magnetic tape, each learner's poster board, and scissors.*

Review all of the Faith Traits: *generosity, loyalty, wisdom, stewardship, obedience, humility, thankfulness, compassion, empathy, peace,* and *joy*. **Our Faith Trait today is thankfulness, a word we have already had, and it is a good reminder that we always have a lot for which to be thankful!** Have the learners attach the Faith Trait sticker to the poster board next to the space where they cut out their last piece. Help them cut the poster board around the shape of the sticker and attach a strip of magnetic tape to the back. Encourage learners to add their piece to their puzzle at home. Review the Big Idea for this session.

Live the Story (25 minutes)

Ways to Witness

M&P *Each learner will need Leaflet 14 (LR) and crayons or markers.*

Invite the learners to look at the next leaflet page and find "I Am Thankful for My Family." **Each one of us has a family. Let's share something about our families with each other. Turn to the person next to you and talk about your family. How many people are in your family? Does your family have pets? What does your family like to do together?** After pairs have shared, encourage, but do not force, the children to share a few of the things they said. Then read the activity aloud. Give the learners time to draw their families (including their pets!) in the space.

Kids Create (Choose One!)

M&P *Celebrate Wind Socks: You will need one 9" x 18" (23 cm x 46 cm) sheet of construction paper for each learner, as well as the crepe paper streamers from "Story Fire-Up." You will also need a paper punch, yarn, stapler, tape, colorful paper scraps, scissors, and glue.*

Advent Calendars: Copy Reproducible Sheet G (TCK) on heavy paper for each learner. Cut out the block of Advent calendar stickers on Sticker Sheet 1 (LR) to give to each learner.

Celebrate Wind Socks: Invite the learners to use colorful paper scraps and crayons or markers to decorate the sheet of construction paper. When they are finished with their designs, help the learners roll the paper so the shorter sides barely overlap, then tape or staple the edges together. Punch three holes evenly around the top of the wind sock and tie a length of yarn through each hole. Bring the three pieces of yarn together into the center and tie them together for hanging. Staple the streamers at the bottom of the wind sock all around the edge. **Hang these wind socks outside or in a window to remind others of the joyous Christmas season!**

Advent Calendar: Distribute the reproducible sheet you copied. Help learners follow the directions to make an Advent calendar. Talk with the learners about the season. **Advent is a time of waiting until the birthday of Jesus on Christmas Day. This calendar can help you count the days and weeks until Christmas comes! Each day of Advent, put the correct number sticker on the number in the correct picture. This will help you count the days until Jesus' birth!**

Wrapping It Up

M&P *You will need the Witness CD (TCK) and a CD player.*

Invite the learners to join you in a circle. **Think about all that you have to be thankful for!** Play Track 14 of the CD as a review of the Bible story. Remind the learners to share their projects and the activities on the leaflet's back page with their families at home. Close with prayer. **Thank you, Lord, for this day and for all of my friends at Sunday school! Thank you for this church and for all of the people here who love and care for us. Help us to be helpful this week in everything that we do. Amen**

Teacher Boost

How did you show thankfulness for each child in your class today? Were you able to enjoy and appreciate each one, even those who seem to have so much energy it makes you tired just to look at them? Remember that each child is a special and loved child of God!

Witnesses in the World

It would be fun to plan a party for next session to share with family members or caregivers. Perhaps another class could join with you to create an "open house" of joy. If you do this, make a simple invitation or call all families during the week to personally invite them. It would be best not to disrupt the entire session but to have a party during the last 10 minutes of class time.

GREAT good byes

Give a special good-bye to any guests or visitors, inviting them to come back next time. As you say good-bye to all of the children, remind them to be thankful.

Jesus Is Born

Bible Text

Luke 2:1-20

Key Verse

To you is born this day in the city of David a Savior, who is the Messiah, the Lord. Luke 2:11

Jesus is the best gift ever!

Session at a Glance	What You Need	What Learners Do
Ready for the Story (15 minutes)		
Welcome the Witnesses	• Christmas music CD, CD player	• Listen to a CD.
Story Warm-Up	• Building blocks	• Build a stable and the town of Bethlehem.
Story Fire-Up	• Plastic straws, construction paper, scissors, glitter glue, stapler	• Make a star wand.
Explore the Story (20 minutes)		
Story Set-Up	• Leaflet 15 (LR), Sticker Sheet 2 (LR), Activity Card D (TCK), Poster K (TCK), removable tape, crayons or markers	• Complete the maze.
Storytelling	• Leaflet 15 (LR), Activity Card C (TCK), Witness CD (TCK), Poster A (TCK), CD player	• Learn the Bible story about Jesus' birth.
Faith Traits	• Sticker Sheet 1 (LR), magnetic tape, poster board, scissors	• Learn about the Faith Trait of harmony.
Live the Story (25 minutes)		
Ways to Witness	• Leaflet 15 (LR), crayons or markers	• Think about ways to share the good news.
Kids Create	• Activity Card C (TCK), white paper, heavy paper, shoe boxes, crayons or markers, scissors, glue, craft sticks • White paper, craft foam or cardboard, white paint, dark blue or black construction paper, paint shirts, hand wipes or water and paper towels	• Make nativity dioramas. • Make angel prints.
Wrapping It Up	• Witness CD (TCK), CD player	• Review the Bible story.

LR = Learner Resource
TCK = Teacher Class Kit
M&P = Materials and Preparation

What Factors Shaped This Story?

The Roman Empire dominated the Mediterranean at the time of Jesus' birth. The people bore a heavy economic and political burden. Local Jewish government was beholden to Roman patronage. The registration witnessed in this passage was not only a census. A government undertook a census for particular reasons, including taxation and military conscription. Though Jesus was not conceived as Joseph's child, Joseph's fatherhood associates the child with the lineage of King David from which was to come a deliverer. Shepherds were outcast because their occupation was unclean and because of their wandering in and out of communities.

What Is This Story About?

Joseph and Mary obeyed the law and went to their hometown. Because of the census, the town's accommodations were crowded. Perhaps also because of the couple's meager means, they found rest in a stable, where Jesus was born. Outside the town, shepherds learned of this birth. A divine messenger, shining in the night, came to them with the news. The shepherds were terrified! The messenger comforted them and told them to find more reassurance in the child. Soon other heavenly voices joined the messenger in heavenly song. The shepherds went as they had been told and, having seen the child, told others.

Why Is This Story Important?

As the world's powers make decrees from capital cities, people go about living their lives. During an emperor's reign, in fulfillment of a promise, a new reign is ushered in. A child is born. We may assume the emperor's census counts the child. Meanwhile, in heaven, too, this birth is registered and proclaimed to earth—not to emperors but to shepherds and even sheep on dark hillsides. In Jesus' birth God draws our attention away from the decrees of the powerful toward the pursuits of the lowly. Follow the shepherds to see what heaven proclaims that is yet unnoticed by the world's powers.

Age-Level Connection

Is there any better time to be with young children than at Christmas? Their joy is contagious! There is joy in everything that takes place during this time of year. Help them to see that their words and actions can be the best gift that people receive this year!

Teacher Prayer

Lord, as I finish this semester with these children, I pray that I have been a witness to your love each time I have been with them. Help me to share the good news of your love as we celebrate the birth of your Son, Jesus. Amen

Question for Reflection

In what special ways will you share the good news with others this Christmas season?

Learner Goals

KNOW

Jesus is their Savior

GROW

in understanding that they can share the good news with others

SHOW

joy as children of God

FACTOID

Beginning with Julius Caesar in 100 B.C., *emperor* or *caesar* was the title for rulers of the Roman Empire.

WORDS

harmony, Bethlehem, good news

FACTOID

Behind the word *angel* (Luke 2:9) is the Greek word for "messenger" and behind *host* (Luke 2:13) is the Greek word for "army."

▶ Transition Tip ◀

Play Christmas music as a transition for each activity today. See if the learners can "name that tune" as you play a portion of it.

Ready for the Story (15 minutes)

Welcome the Witnesses

M&P *You will need a Christmas music CD and a CD player. Play the music as the children arrive.*

Welcome everyone who comes today, especially anyone who has been gone for a time. **Merry Christmas! What do you like to do with your family for Christmas?**

Story Warm-Up

M&P *Set out building blocks.*

Encourage the learners to join in building a stable and the town of Bethlehem. Talk about building as they work, asking about some of the different kinds of buildings they have seen. **Have you been in a tall building? Have you been in a building with an elevator? Have you been in an underground building? Have you been in a barn? Do you know what kind of building you were born in? I bet no one was born in a stable like baby Jesus was!**

Story Fire-Up

M&P *Cut a large star out of construction paper for each child. Gather a plastic straw for each child, glitter glue, and a stapler. Make a sample star wand by drawing glitter glue squiggles or lines on a star you cut out. Staple the star to a straw to make a wand.*

Show the learners your star wand and invite each of them to make a wand of his or her own. **This special star wand is a reminder of the stars that shone the night that Jesus was born. As we talk about Jesus today, wave your star wand in the air.**

Explore the Story (20 minutes)

Story Set-Up

M&P *Gather Leaflet 15 from the Pre-Kindergarten/Kindergarten Learner Resource (LR) and the angel sticker from Sticker Sheet 2 (LR). Have crayons or markers available. Display Poster K from the Age 2–Grade 4 Teacher Class Kit (TCK) and have the Session 15 Big Idea sentence strip from Activity Card D (TCK) and removable tape available. Remove the Session 14 sentence strip from the poster and display it somewhere in the classroom.*

Ask one of the learners to hand out the leaflets. Look together at the front. Read the directions and complete the maze to help the shepherds find their way to the stable. When they have completed the maze, have them add the angel sticker above the stable. Review the Big Ideas that have been presented this semester, using the sentence strips you have displayed in the classroom. Introduce the Big Idea for today, found on the back of the leaflet. **Jesus is the best gift ever!** Invite a learner to tape the Big Idea sentence strip to the space on Poster K. **Isn't it great that God gave us Jesus? What great gift have you gotten for your birthday or Christmas?** Encourage everyone to share.

Storytelling

M&P *Listen to Track 15 of the Witness CD (TCK) and decide whether to use it to tell the Bible story. You will need a CD player and Leaflet 15 (LR). Display Poster A (TCK) so everyone can see it. Decide whether you will use the story figures on side 2 of Activity Card C (TCK) as part of the story.*

Have the learners open their leaflets and talk about what they see in the Bible story picture. Direct their attention to Poster A. Point out Mary, Joseph, the angels, and the shepherds. Tell the Bible story, either reading it from the leaflet or playing Track 15 of the CD, using the story figures from the activity card. After telling the story, allow time for the learners to act it out if they wish. Talk about any Christmas programs or movies they may have seen. **How do you think Mary and Joseph felt? If you had been a shepherd, how would you have felt when the angels sang? Would you have gone to the stable? We are so glad that Jesus was born! Jesus is the best gift ever!**

FAITH Traits

M&P *You will need the Session 15 Faith Trait sticker on Sticker Sheet 1 (LR), magnetic tape, each learner's poster board, and scissors.*

Today's Faith Trait is harmony. Harmony is when things come together in a pleasing way, like in music. When the angels sang on the night of Jesus' birth, the harmony must have been amazing! Have the learners attach the Faith Trait sticker to the poster board next to the space where they cut out their last piece. Help them cut the poster board around the shape of the sticker and attach a strip of magnetic tape to the back. Encourage learners to add this last piece to their puzzle at home. **Do you know what shape the Faith Traits magnet puzzle makes? A heart! This heart will remind you how much God loves you!** Talk about the great gifts the learners have received and about some of the gifts they hope they get this Christmas. Then repeat together today's Big Idea. **Jesus is the best gift ever!**

Kid Connect

Children love birthday celebrations, and they will relate to the excitement of Jesus' birthday. Some families celebrate Jesus' birthday in a special way by having a birthday cake. Help the learners to realize that Jesus' birthday changed the world forever and, as people who love Jesus, we should share that news with others.

More Movement

Play a game of Freeze Tag as characters from the Christmas story. For example, have the learners pretend to be angels, then stop in whatever position they are in when you say "Freeze!" Use the characters of Mary, Joseph, the shepherds, and even some of the animals that may have been in the stable with Mary and Joseph on the night of Jesus' birth.

Teacher Boost

Will you return to spend the next semester with the learners or is this your last session with them? If you will return, wish them a Merry Christmas and say that you will look forward to seeing them next year. If this is your last session with the learners, say a special good-bye and that you will look for them in church.

Witnesses in the World

Bring supplies to put together Christmas stockings for people who are homeless. Purchase a bulk package of calf-length sports socks and have learners add an orange to each toe, as well as small toiletry items, a candy bar, pack of gum or cards, or other items anyone would enjoy. Find a shelter where you could donate these stockings, and know that people will have a better Christmas as they use the items in the stockings and have a new pair of socks to wear.

GREAT good byes

Give each learner a hug as he or he leaves and make sure each has all of the projects from the semester. **Jesus is the best gift ever!**

Live the Story (25 minutes)

Ways to Witness

M&P *Each learner will need Leaflet 15 (LR) and crayons or markers.*

Have the learners turn to the next page in their leaflets and look at "Sharing the Good News!" **Look at the pictures on this page. Does each picture show someone sharing the good news of God's love? Draw a circle around the pictures that show someone sharing the good news of God's love.** Give learners time to complete the task. **What are some ways we can share the good news of God's love with others?**

Kids Create (Choose One!)

M&P *Nativity Diorama: Trace the outlines of the story figures on Activity Card C Side 2 (TCK) onto a sheet of white paper. Copy this sheet onto heavy paper, one per learner. Each learner will also need a shoe box. You will need crayons or markers, scissors, glue, and craft sticks.*

Angel Print: Draw a simple angel outline on a sheet of craft foam or cardboard and cut it out. You will need white paint, dark blue or black construction paper the same size as the paper angel shape, paint shirts, and hand wipes or water and paper towels.

Nativity Diorama: Give each learner the copy of the figures you traced and encourage them to color and cut them out. Attach each figure to a craft stick with a thin line of glue. Explain that the box will rest on one of its long sides, and the bottom of the box will be the back of the scene. Have the learners decorate their boxes inside to resemble a stable or barn. Cut slits in the boxes for the children. **You can stick your figures through the slits and tell others the story of Jesus' birth!**

Angel Print: Show the learners the angel shape and explain that they can make many angel prints using this one pattern. Paint the foam or cardboard angel shape with white paint, then press it carefully onto blue or black paper. Peel it up to reveal the angel print. Set the prints aside to dry.

Wrapping It Up

M&P *You will need the Witness CD (TCK) and a CD player.*

Be sure to include the learners in any cleanup that needs to be done from all of the session activities. Review the Bible story of the first Christmas. **Jesus is the best gift ever! Remember that no matter what gifts you get for Christmas, you've already received the best one!** Replay Track 15 of the CD to hear the Christmas story again if you have time. Point out the fun activities on the back of the leaflet, and remind the learners to add their Faith Trait magnet to the puzzle they have at home. Close with this prayer. **Thank you, God, for the best gift you could ever give us: your Son, Jesus. Help us to always share the good news with people everywhere. Amen**

What Are Bonus Sessions?

The five Bonus sessions during each semester of Witness offer theme-based learning opportunities in a shorter, particularly flexible format. Bonus sessions provide additional content for Sunday school programs that need more than 15 sessions per semester. They can also be used when teachers want experiential learning with a different pace.

What Is the Content of Bonus Sessions?

Bonus sessions offer the same set of categories represented by different Bible stories in each semester. In the Jesus' Teachings category, learners take a look at one or more of Jesus' teachings. Learners make Old Testament/New Testament Connections when they compare and contrast related Old and New Testament texts. Each semester, learners can take a Field Trip to explore a space outside of the classroom. A Seasonal Preparations session is offered each semester to provide an additional session on Advent (Semester 1) or Lent (Semester 2). Bonus sessions in the Worship category provide a time for learners to investigate faith practices and worship styles.

When Should I Use Bonus Sessions?

Bonus sessions can be plugged into the schedule at any time. If you have one, the Sunday school coordinator should coordinate group plans, especially related to Seasonal Preparations. Ask your Sunday school planner if Bonus sessions across age and grade levels will be planned for the same day, or if you have flexibility in scheduling them. If you are doing your own planning, browse through the Bonus sessions to see which ones you'd like to use and when.

What Are the Parts of a Bonus Session?

The first page of each Bonus session gets teachers and kids ready to learn. Pre-class preparation helps for the teacher, and one or more Ready for the Story activities for kids launch the Bible story investigations. The second page provides Explore the Story and Live the Story options for digging into the Bible story and making life applications. Some of the same sidebar headings from Core sessions are included in Bonus sessions.

What Do Learners Use during Bonus Sessions?

The learner resource for the Bonus sessions has two parts, neither of which is part of the Core learner resource. Each Bonus session has one reproducible page printed in the teacher guide and one reproducible sheet found in the teacher class kit. Be sure to make arrangements for timely and efficient photocopying of the appropriate pages and sheets for your group.

God Blesses Everyone!

Bible Text

Matthew 5:1-12

Key Verse

Blessed are the peacemakers, for they will be called children of God. Matthew 5:9

Jesus blesses us.

M&P

READY FOR THE STORY
Copy Repro Page A (page 92) for each learner. Gather crayons or markers. Have the Witness CD (TCK) and a CD player available.

Bible Background

In Matthew, Jesus gave five major speeches. The first was the Sermon on the Mount (chapters 5–7). Jesus began teaching his followers about the way of life in the kingdom of God. As his followers, they would have a new way of life. In Luke 6:17-49, we find the Sermon on the Plain. Like the sermon in Matthew, it was named for its site. Matthew and Luke include similar, but differing, renditions of the Beatitudes. The Sermon on the Mount also includes teaching on Jewish law, giving alms, prayer, fasting, wealth, and other matters of faith.

The Beatitudes proclaim the blessedness of those who live according to God's ways. These are part of the way of life in God's coming kingdom or reign, which Jesus proclaims. Each beatitude proclaims who are blessed and the blessing they shall receive. The first eight refer to the blessed in the third person. The ninth uses the second person—you. In the ninth, Matthew is speaking directly to the church. Believers can expect persecution for being followers of Jesus. The Beatitudes focus on the blessing or happiness of God's reign by contrast to life according to the world.

The form of these sayings would have been familiar to many people listening. Such sayings of blessedness were common in the Greek environment of Jesus' day. The usual pattern was celebrating people who had achieved worldly success or something desirable, such as wealth, wisdom, or a happy family. Jesus' beatitudes do not celebrate people's accomplishments but proclaim the reign of God that is coming. Jesus' blessings announce a future that turns the world upside down.

Ready for the Story (20 minutes)

Jumping Our Blessings: God blesses all of us with our families who love us, the things we like to do and are good at, and lots, lots more. What blessings has God given you? Allow time for answers. **Did you do anything to receive your blessings? God gives us blessings without us having to do anything! Let's count our blessings as we jump in place!** Explain that learners will jump once and name one of their blessings. Then they'll jump twice and name another blessing, and so on. **Wow! God has blessed us with so much!** Hand out the repro page and read the directions aloud. The learners will draw pictures of four of their special blessings from these categories: people, food, home, Jesus. As learners work, play the Witness Theme Song (Track 16). Encourage them to listen to the words and begin to learn the song.

Explore the Story (15 minutes)

Blessed by God: Explore and explain several of the Beatitudes. Here are simplified explanations of the Beatitudes with movement to help the learners begin to understand what they mean.

Blessed are those who feel compassion, for they will go to heaven. *(Make sad faces, then happy faces.)*

Blessed are those who ask for forgiveness, for they will be hugged. *(Pretend to cry, then hug yourself.)*

Blessed are those who are gentle, for they will have what they need. *(Gently pat the shoulder of a person near you, then jump for joy.)*

Blessed are those who act fairly, for God will fill them with love. *(Pretend to share something with another person near you, then place your hands over your heart.)*

Blessed are those who care for others, for they will be cared for. *(Pat one another on the back.)*

Blessed are those who act like Jesus, for they will be close to God. *(Pretend to pray.)*

Blessed are those who are peacemakers, for they will be children of God. *(Shake hands with one another.)*

Blessed are those who stand up for what is right, for they will go to heaven. *(Stand up straight, then point to heaven.)*

Repeat this activity several times so learners know the actions. Then say the Beatitudes (with motions) quietly, then whispering, then with just the motions.

Live the Story (25 minutes)

Smile: How can you show caring for others? *(Allow time for answers.)* **One of the easiest ways to show you care is to smile at someone. A smile makes you and the other person feel happy. Smiling is a way to show others that God loves them!** Smile at the learners and see what happens. Invite them to smile at one another. **You can make others happy just by giving them your caring smile.** Have the learners draw smiles on five index cards and put their name on the backs. Discuss with them who they could give their "smiles" to. *(Answers might include Mom, Dad, Grandma, Grandpa, neighbors.)* Clip each learner's "smiles" together for the children to take home.

I Care: What are other ways we can show others we care? *(Donating toys, clothes, and other items to a shelter; donating food to a food bank; volunteering as a family at a soup kitchen, and so on.)* Complete the dot-to-dot of the dove at the top of Reproducible Sheet K. **That bird is a dove. Sometimes a dove is used to show peace. What does the word** *peace* **mean?** Allow time for answers. **It means that there is no fighting, that we feel cared for and happy. When we smile at someone and do other things to show we care, we are helping that person to feel peace.**

A Special Place: Hand out a sheet of 11" x 14" (28 cm x 36 cm) construction paper to each learner. **Think of someone in your family whom you care about. Draw some ways you can show them you care on your sheet of paper. We're making placemats so that person can have a special place at the table during meals.** Allow learners time to work. As they finish, affix the clear adhesive paper to both sides of each placemat. Trim off any excess.

Closing Prayer: Dear Jesus, thank you for blessing me with so much. Please help me to share my blessings to help care for others. Amen

M&P

EXPLORE THE STORY
You will need space to move around.

LIVE THE STORY
You will need crayons or markers, index cards, paper clips, a copy of Reproducible Sheet K (TCK) for each learner, 11" x 14" (28 cm x 36 cm) construction paper, and clear adhesive paper.

Learner Goals

KNOW
God blesses them

GROW
in compassion for others who are less fortunate

SHOW
kindness to those around them

Teacher Prayer

Dear Lord, help me to show mercy and compassion, encourage me to be pure in heart, and help me to thirst for hunger and righteousness. Above all, help me show my learners how to do the same. Amen

Question for Reflection

How do I show compassion for others?

Leaders of the Bible Have Faith!

Bible Text

Hebrews 11:1-31

Key Verse

Now faith is the assurance of things hoped for, the conviction of things not seen. Hebrews 11:1

BIG Idea

We belong to a family of faith.

M&P

READY FOR THE STORY
You will need blindfolds, crayons or markers, and a copy of Repro Page B (page 93) for each learner. Have the Witness CD (TCK) and a CD player available.

Bible Background

Hebrews' audience is Jews who have recognized Jesus as the Messiah and have become Christian. The letter focuses on Jesus' superiority to all that have gone before. It teaches the superiority of salvation in Jesus Christ compared to a system of laws and sacrifices. The writer is encouraging believers to persevere in their faith against the temptation to go back to their former practices or to another person as messiah. The writer exhorts the people to faith.

Chapter 11 describes faith as "the assurance of things hoped for, the conviction of things not seen" (11:1) and provides a roll call of exemplars in faith. They are models standing as witnesses and encouragement to believers. The author of Hebrews describes important figures in Jewish tradition as having anticipated Jesus by faith. They had faith but did not have the final fulfillment of seeing all that had been promised. In faith they continued to believe in what they had not seen.

Christianity began among first-century Jews who believed that Jesus was the long-expected Messiah. What was the relationship between the faith and practices that had been theirs as Jews and the new life and faith they were learning in Jesus? Rather than be cut off from the long tradition of the faithful, they came to understand following Jesus as a renewal of their faith that required a new understanding of their past. For Christians today, this means that we have a long lineage of models whose example can inspire and sustain us in our faith.

Ready for the Story (20 minutes)

Walk of Faith: We will have popcorn at the end of the session today. How do you know there will be popcorn? Can you see it? Can you smell it? *(Make sure that they cannot.)* **You'll have to have faith in my word. What is faith?** *(Believing in something you cannot see, such as God; trusting another person.)* **Who do you know who has faith?** *(Parents, grandparents, pastors, and so on.)* **How do you know they have faith?** *(They pray and talk about their faith.)* **We're going to take a faith walk with a friend.** Separate the class into pairs. Each person in the pair takes a turn being blindfolded. The one who can see leads the other around the room very carefully. If any learners are uncomfortable being blindfolded, have them close their eyes. **How did it feel to have faith in another person?** Allow time for answers. Hand out the repro page and explain the activity to the learners. **Color in the dotted spaces to discover a word.** Allow learners time to work. **Do you know what it is?** *(Accept responses.)* **The word is** *faith.*

Play the Witness Theme Song (Track 16) and encourage learners to dance to the music as they listen to the words of the song.

Explore the Story (20 minutes)

Great Leaders, Great Faith: Remember that we're having popcorn later, even though you can't see or smell it, so you must have faith. Some of the great people in the Bible had faith in God. Talk about the following people and have the learners act out a part of each story.

■ **Noah believed when God told him that God was going to destroy the earth. Noah had faith and built a boat where there was no water. Pretend to build a boat like Noah.**

■ **Abraham went where God told him to go even though he didn't know where he was going. He had faith that God would lead him to the right place. Abraham also believed when God told him that he would have a child. He had faith even though he and his wife were very old. Walk around like you are traveling like Abraham; rock a baby in your arms.**

■ **Moses obeyed God's laws. He had faith that God's laws were right. Other people were disobeying but Moses did not. Pretend to read God's laws like Moses.**

■ **The Israelites passed through the Red Sea because God told them they would be safe. The Israelites had faith in God. Walk through the Red Sea like the Israelites. Watch out for the water around you!**

Respect is our faith trait for today. When we respect someone, we think very well of them. We are showing respect to Noah, Abraham, Moses, and the Israelites because we are talking about and remembering them. How else can we show respect to someone?

Live the Story (20 minutes)

Popcorn: Invite learners to hand out napkins and pour a little popcorn on their napkins. As they eat their popcorn, discuss the following questions. **Did you believe that I would give you popcorn? How did you know? You had faith in what I told you. Who else do you have faith in?** *(Parents, grandparents, aunts, uncles, friends, and so on.)* **You also have a special faith in God. If you believe that God loves you, you have faith!** Remind learners about the people they learned about earlier in the session who had faith in God. Have them draw a picture of one of these people in the box on the reproducible sheet. After they are done drawing, help write the name of the person they drew on the line after the text, "*(Child's name)*'s faith is like _____."

Talking Faith: Invite a pastor to visit your class to talk about what it means for him or her to have faith in God. When did he or she know he or she first had faith? Who do the learners know in the congregation who have great faith, and how do they know this? Encourage the learners to ask the pastor questions.

Faith Rocks: Give each learner a Faith Rock and set out the paint supplies. Encourage learners to decorate their rocks, painting around, but not over, the word FAITH. Set them aside to dry. **Keep your Faith Rock in your pocket to remind you that your faith in God is as solid as a rock.**

Closing Prayer: Dear God, thank you for everyone who has faith in you. So many people love you! I'm so glad that you're in my heart. Amen

M&P

EXPLORE THE STORY
You will need a Bible and space to move about.

LIVE THE STORY
Make popcorn before class. Place the popcorn in an airtight container so the scent is not detectable. Before serving any food, always check with caregivers for learners who have food allergies. Provide an alternative if necessary. Gather napkins, crayons or markers, and a copy of Reproducible Sheet L (TCK) for each child. Gather a small rock for each learner, and provide several colors of washable paint, painbrushes, and small cups of water. Paint the word FAITH on each rock.

Learner Goals

KNOW

the stories of biblical figures who had great faith

GROW

in faith in God

SHOW

faith in each other

Teacher Prayer

Dear Lord, help me to demonstrate the faith of those we read about in the Bible and to be sure of things that are not seen. Help me to pass this faith on to the learners so they might know your great love. Amen

Question for Reflection

What can I do to strengthen my faith during the difficult times that test it?

High Fives to God!

Bible Text

Psalms 45; 51; 92; 98; 119

Key Verse

O sing to the Lord a new song, for [God] has done marvelous things. Psalm 98:1

We can praise and thank God.

M&P

READY FOR THE STORY

For Station 1 (Smell): Pour small amounts of cooking flavors in uninflated nonlatex balloons, inflate, and tie. For Station 2 (Touch): Choose an object the learners will recognize (like a small doll or car) and place it inside a paper bag. For Station 3 (Sight): Gather from magazines pictures that are pleasing and not pleasing to God. For Station 4 (Hearing): Locate a CD of noise, instruments, or animals. For Station 5 (Taste): Choose a variety of unusual fruits or vegetables and cut them into bite-sized pieces. Before serving any food, always check with caregivers for learners who have food allergies. Provide an alternative if necessary. Have the Witness CD (TCK) and a CD player available.

Bible Background

The word *psalm* means hymn or song. Psalms are used in worship. They express varied human relationships to God, including praise, thanksgiving, and lament. Some tell stories of God's presence with the people through history, express trust in God's faithfulness, or explore God's word and ways. Some are used for particular celebrations or types of worship. Psalms express virtually all human emotions that come to us bodily through our five senses as well as through our thoughts.

In Psalms 92 and 98, hear the lute, harp, human voice, lyres, trumpets, horns, sea, floods, and singing hills. To what other senses do these psalms refer? Psalm 119 meditates on God's teaching, using many different words including *law, decrees, ways, precepts,* and *statutes.* (That's only through verse 5!) How do our five senses contribute to our knowledge of God's teaching? Besides sight and hearing, notice touch, smell, and taste in Psalm 51 and listen for the sound of God in Psalm 45.

Human beings are physical creatures. We know God through our bodies. All our senses can be attuned to God's presence and we can use our human capacities to let others know about God through their senses. Just as we see, hear, taste, touch, and smell God, we can help others see God in our actions, hear God in our words, taste and smell God in our meals, and touch God in our careful and peaceful dealings with one another.

Ready for the Story (20 minutes)

Exploring Our Senses: Explore the five senses with five sensory stations. (Be sensitive throughout the session to learners who may not have the use of all their senses.) This can be done as a whole group or in small groups with adult helpers.

- *Station 1 (Smell):* Learners smell the balloons and try to guess each scent.
- *Station 2 (Touch):* Learners put a hand inside the paper bag without looking inside and try to identify what the item is.
- *Station 3 (Sight):* Learners sort pictures of things that are pleasing to God and those things that might not be pleasing to God.
- *Station 4 (Hearing):* Learners listen to a recording of different noises, instruments, farm animals, and so on and try to identify each sound.
- *Station 5 (Taste):* Learners taste different fruits and vegetables that you cut up. Encourage them to taste, but do not force anyone to do so.

Play the Witness Theme Song (Track 16) and encourage learners to sing along as they learn the words to the song.

Explore the Story (15 minutes)

Sing Praise to God: Sing the hymn "Earth and All Stars" (*Lutheran Book of Worship* 558). **This song praises God. Do you know another song that praises God? The Psalms is like a book of songs. Sometimes we sing parts of them while we're in church. I'm going to read a few psalms to you. See if you can guess which sense each psalm is talking about. If you know, point to that sense on your body.** Read Psalm 92:1-4, 11; 98:1, 4-9; 119:12-18, 103, 145-149; 45:7-11; and 51:8, 14-15. Help the learners to guess the sense if they are struggling to figure it out.

Live the Story (25 minutes)

High Fives to God: How can we praise God with all of our senses? Make a picture chart of the five senses (*smell: nose; touch: hand; taste: mouth; hearing: ear; sight: eye*). Invite learners to think of different things they can do to praise God using their five senses. Have them indicate which sense their ideas use by pointing to the correct sense picture on the chart. Every time a learner contributes, give that child a high five. **You can think about a "high five" to God as using your five senses to praise God every day.** Distribute Repro Page C. Read the directions aloud and allow learners time to work. **Who remembers what it means to be generous?** (*To give of yourself and your belongings freely.*) **How can using your five senses help you to be generous?** Allow time for answers.

Five Senses Collage: Encourage learners to look through magazines to find pictures of people using their five senses. Have them glue the picture on the chart under the sense the image represents. The chart will then become a collage of praise with the five senses.

A High Five: Distribute the construction paper, one sheet per learner. Help learners trace both of their hands on the paper. Encourage them to decorate each hand with crayons, markers, and glitter glue. Help learners cut out each paper hand as they finish. **Give these "high fives" to friends or family members. Share with them how they can praise God using their five senses and give a "high five" to God.**

As learners leave today, give each a "high five" to remind him or her of the session. Give each learner Reproducible Sheet M to use at home.

Closing Prayer: Dear God, I'm giving you a high five! You are so good to me. Help me to praise you with my five senses and to show others how to praise you with their five senses. Amen

M&P

EXPLORE THE STORY
You will need *Lutheran Book of Worship* and a Bible.

LIVE THE STORY
You will need a copy of Repro Page C (page 94) and Reproducible Sheet M (TCK) for each learner, chart paper, crayons or markers, magazines, scissors, construction paper, and glitter glue.

Learner Goals

KNOW
their five senses

GROW
in awareness of all those things that are pleasing to God

SHOW
others how to use their senses to praise God

Teacher Prayer

Dear Lord, today let me use my voice for teaching and praising you, my eyes to see the good in all the learners, my hands to do good works, my ears to hear the learners praise you, and my nose to smell the wonders you have created. Amen

Question for Reflection

Do I praise God with all of my senses?

Be Patient

Bible Text

Luke 1:5-25

Key Verse

But the angel said to him, "Do not be afraid, Zechariah, for your prayer has been heard. Your wife Elizabeth will bear you a son, and you will name him John. You will have joy and gladness, and many will rejoice at his birth." Luke 1:13-14

BIG Idea

God answers prayers.

M&P

READY FOR THE STORY

You will need a cookie recipe, cookie ingredients, baking supplies, an oven, and napkins. Have the ingredients and supplies out and ready to go. Decide ahead of time what steps your learners will be able to do. Before serving any food, always check with caregivers for learners who have food allergies. Provide an alternative if necessary. Have the Witness CD (TCK) and a CD player available.

Bible Background

John was Jesus' cousin. The mothers Elizabeth and Mary were relatives (1:36). In some ways, John and Jesus were similar. John's birth, like Jesus', was extraordinary. Both John and Jesus baptized. Indeed, John baptized Jesus (3:21-22). Yet John made clear Jesus' priority over himself in his proclamation. John was Jesus' forerunner, proclaiming and preparing the way for Jesus (3:3-6, 16-17).

Zechariah and Elizabeth diligently practiced their faith and observed God's ways. Zechariah, from a priestly family, was serving in the Jerusalem temple when God's messenger told him that he and Elizabeth would have a son though Elizabeth was barren and past childbearing age. The child would be like the prophet Elijah and would prepare the people for the Lord. Zechariah doubted the prophecy. Until the time of the child's naming (1:64), he was made mute, which told people that something amazing was happening. Indeed, Elizabeth conceived a child!

Zechariah and Elizabeth were unsuspecting, surprised recipients of God's gift of a child. In the proclamation of John's birth, God was unfolding a plan. John's birth and making "ready a people prepared for the Lord" (1:17) was part of God's making way for coming in Jesus Christ. God continues to make way for Jesus in our lives. God used means that may have seemed impossible, like people such as Zechariah and Elizabeth, who seemed too old, or like John, who may have seemed too young.

Ready for the Story (20 minutes)

Let's Make Cookies!: What is hard to wait for? *(Answers may include parents coming home from work, birthdays, Christmas, special trip or vacation, or cookies to bake.)* **Why do you have a hard time waiting for these things?**

Today we're going to make cookies! Make a simple batch of cookies with the learners' help. Each child could add an ingredient, give the batch a stir, or some other task. Have an adult helper put the cookies in an oven. Continue with the session while the cookies are baking. **Is it hard or easy to wait for the cookies to bake and then to cool? How many of you know what the word** *patience* **means?** Allow time for answers. **Patience is our faith trait for today. Being patient means waiting without getting upset, worried, or anxious. In the Bible story for today people had to wait and have patience for a long time.** Plan to enjoy the cookies with the learners at the end of the session.

Play the Witness Theme Song (Track 16) and invite learners to think of actions to go along with the song.

Explore the Story (15 minutes)

Read aloud the Bible story. **In the story today, Zechariah and his wife Elizabeth had been praying for a child. They were patiently waiting for an answer to their prayer. Have you ever prayed for anything? God always hears and answers our prayers. Sometimes God doesn't always give us the answer we were hoping for. But God has a plan and will answer our prayers in a way that is best for us.**

Elizabeth and Zechariah had to be patient for a long time for John to be born and have a birthday. When are your birthdays? For those learners who may not know theirs, refer to your list. Help the learners sit in a circle in the order of their birthdays. **Is it difficult to be patient and wait for your birthday to come? Starting from today, whose birthday is first? Who has to wait the longest for their birthday? What can you do to help yourself be patient as you wait for your birthday?**

Live the Story (25 minutes)

Thank You, God!: Do any of you say prayers before you go to bed? Do any of you pray before you eat? Praying is a way for us to talk to God. In a prayer, we can thank God for everything we have, ask questions of God, and talk to God like you would talk to your mom or dad. As a class, write a simple prayer using pictures to illustrate what your class is thankful for, could improve in, would wish for (not toys), and who they would like God to bless. Draw your prayer on a chalkboard or chart paper. Pray the prayer together as a class.

My Prayer: Distribute Repro Page D. Encourage learners to create their own prayer by following the directions on the page. Have the learners share the prayers with the class if they wish.

Patience Is Rewarded: Gather the cookies you made in the beginning of the session and give one to each learner. **You did a great job of being patient while the cookies were baking! These cookies were worth waiting for. So is everything else God gives us.** Hand out the reproducible sheet and encourage learners to do the activities on the sheets with their families.

Closing Prayer: Dear God, thank you for the miracle of Jesus. Help me to be like Elizabeth and Zechariah and have patience for things I may be excited or anxious about. I know you'll take care of me. Amen

M&P

EXPLORE THE STORY
You will need a Bible and a list of the learners' birthdays.

LIVE THE STORY
You will need chart paper, crayons or markers, copies of Reproducible Sheet N and Repro Page D (page 95) for each learner, pencils, and the cookies baked earlier in the session. Before serving any food, always check with caregivers for learners who have food allergies. Provide an alternative if necessary.

Learner Goals

KNOW

what it means to be patient

GROW

in their prayer life with God

SHOW

how to be patient

Teacher Prayer

Dear Lord, help me to have patience with the learners today and to accept them as they are. Help me to teach them about prayer and your wonderful answers to prayer. Give me patience also in my own prayer life. Amen

Question for Reflection

How can I become a more patient person?

Celebrate!

Bible Text

John 2:1-12

Key Verse

Jesus did this, the first of his signs, in Cana of Galilee, and revealed his glory; and his disciples believed in him. John 2:11

Jesus brings joy to all people.

M&P

READY FOR THE STORY
You will need powdered drink mix, two large, clear pitchers, masking tape, a stirring spoon, and water. Before the learners arrive, wrap masking tape around the bottom of one of the clear pitchers, covering a couple of inches, and put a powdered drink mix at the bottom. Fill the other pitcher with water. Have the Witness CD (TCK) and a CD player available.

Bible Background

John's proclamation of Jesus' coming and Jesus' arrival on the scene are found in John 1. The next day Jesus called his first disciples and the following day he began his ministry. At the wedding at Cana, Jesus' actions were the first of many signs by which followers came to believe in him. These events occur at the beginning of The Gospel of John, but the wedding banquet and wine overflowing are often used as images of the final fulfillment of God's relationship with the people.

While Jesus, his mother, and his disciples were at a wedding, the host faced the embarrassment of not enough wine. Jesus' mother brought the problem to him, but his response to her seemed rude, even disrespectful. She trusted that he could address the shortage, and she persisted. Jesus did act, transforming the empty water jars for the rites of purification into jars full of wine for the wedding celebration. In this sign, Jesus' identity began to be revealed and his disciples believed in him.

Often we may think we need to have rock-solid faith before we are worthy or able to follow Jesus. In this story, Mary alone recognizes Jesus' power and believes in him. For the disciples, being with Jesus and witnessing his deeds at the wedding planted the seeds of their belief. Jesus also calls us. This story offers us reassurance that as we follow Jesus, our faith will develop and grow.

Ready for the Story (15 minutes)

It's a Miracle!: Demonstrate the amazing story of Jesus turning the water into wine. (Do not allow the learners to see that there is anything in the pitcher.) **Do you think anything will happen when I pour water into the pitcher?** Add water from another pitcher and watch the learners' amazement as the water turns colorful. Then explain how you performed the "miracle." **How do you think Jesus was able to do miracles?** *(Through God's power.)*

Play the Witness Theme Song (Track 16) several times, encouraging learners to sing along each time, reinforcing the words they know and helping them learn what they don't know. Play it one more time, inviting the learners to create movements as they sing along.

Explore the Story (25 minutes)

Wedding Wine: Tell the following story of the wedding at Cana:

Jesus, his mother Mary, and his disciples were at a wedding banquet at Cana in Galilee. After a while, the supply of wine ran out. Mary told Jesus that the wine had run out. Jesus said, "Why do you ask me? My time has not yet come."

But Mary said to the servants, "Do whatever Jesus tells you to do."

There were six huge stone water jars that were used for washing ceremonies. Jesus told the servants to fill them with water, and they filled the jars. Jesus said, "Now fill a glass and give it to the master of this feast." They did what Jesus asked. The master tasted it and was surprised to taste wine. The water had turned to wine! He had no idea where it came from, but the servants knew. It came from Jesus!

The master said to the groom, "People always drink the best wine first and use the other wine later. But you saved the best wine for last." This was Jesus' first miracle. After that, the disciples believed in him and followed him wherever he went.

Hand out Repro Page E and have the learners follow the directions on the page. **This was the first of the many signs and miracles of Jesus. There was much celebration and much joy. Joy is our faith trait for today. How do you show that you are joyful or happy?** *(Smile, sing, dance, jump, and so on.)* Play some children's praise music and dance around the room for joy! Play Follow the Leader as the music is playing. Have the learners take turns being the leader as they move about the room.

Live the Story (20 minutes)

Joyful Decorations: How do you show that you have the joy of Jesus? *(Sing, dance, pray, come to church, read the Bible, take care of the earth, make new friends, and so on.)* Encourage and suggest other responses if learners are struggling. **We also decorate to celebrate the joy we have in Jesus.** Using some simple birthday decorations such as streamers, pictures, and confetti, invite the learners to decorate the room for Jesus.

Piece of Cake: Hand out Reproducible Sheet O and have the learners decorate the birthday cake in celebration of the joy of Jesus. If time allows use glitter glue and beads as extra decorations on the cake! Encourage the learners to do the activities on the rest of the page with their families.

Celebrate!: Have a small party to celebrate the joy of Jesus. Play some party games: Musical Chairs (using tracks from the Witness CD); Duck, Duck, Goose; and Simon Says. Have the learners return to their seats. Ask a learner to hand out the cups. Pour a little of the drink you made in the beginning of the session in each cup for the learners to enjoy.

Closing Prayer: You are so cool, God! Let me always have the joy of Jesus in my heart and share it with others. Amen

M&P

EXPLORE THE STORY
Have crayons, a CD of children's praise music, a CD player, a copy of Repro Page E (page 96) for each learner, and space to move in.

LIVE THE STORY
You will need simple birthday decorations such as streamers, pictures, and confetti. Provide the drink from "Ready for the Story" and plates, napkins, and cups. Copy Reproducible Sheet O (TCK) for each learner. Before serving any food, always check with caregivers for learners who have food allergies. Provide an alternative if necessary. Have the Witness CD (TCK) and a CD player available.

Learner Goals

KNOW

the story of the wedding at Cana

GROW

in joy in their faith in Jesus

SHOW

others how to celebrate the love of Jesus

Teacher Prayer

Dear Lord, show me how to celebrate the faith I have in you. Help me to demonstrate the joy you bring into my life. Thank you for the joy in my heart! Amen

Question for Reflection

How do I show that I have the joy of Jesus in my heart?

God Blesses Everyone!

Matthew 5:1-12

I am blessed because I am loved.	**I am blessed because I have food to eat.**
I am blessed because I have a place to sleep.	**I am blessed because Jesus loves me!**

Draw a picture of a special blessing in each of the four boxes.

Leaders of the Bible Have Faith!

Hebrews 11:1-31

Color the dotted spaces to reveal a very important word for everyone.

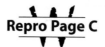

High Fives to God!

Psalms 45; 51; 92; 98; 119

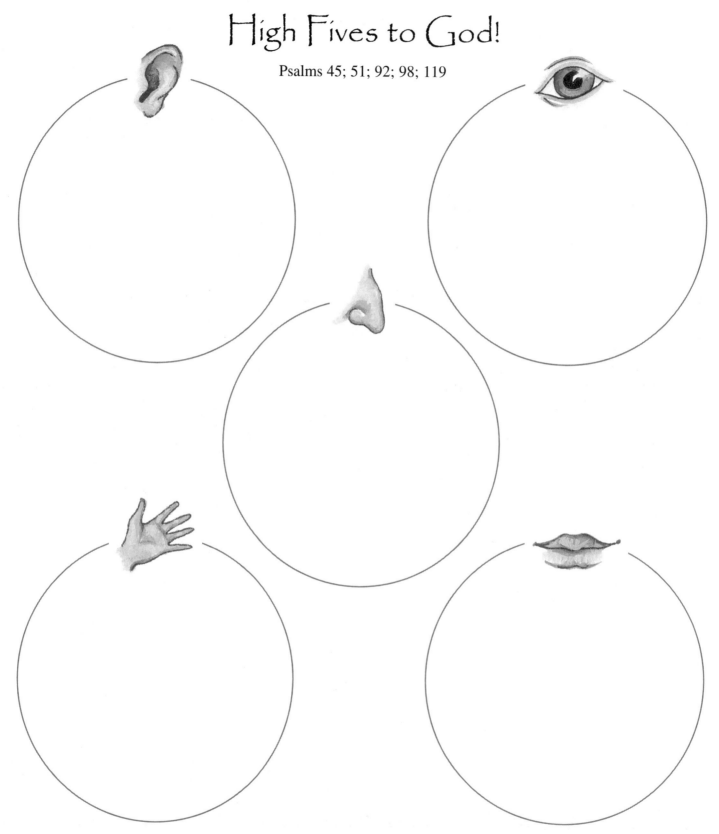

Draw a picture of a way you can praise God using the sense shown in each circle.

Be Patient

Luke 1:5-25

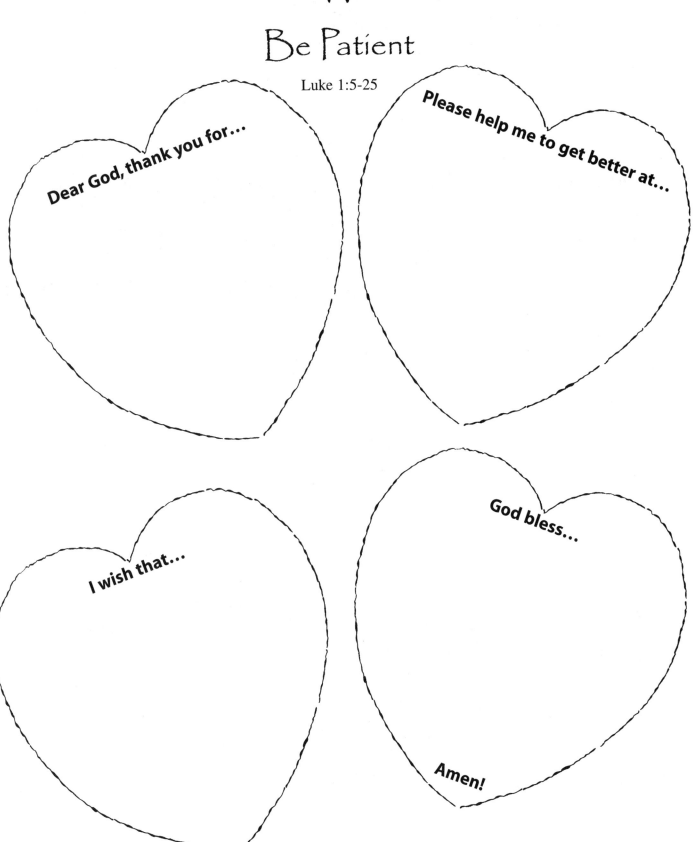

Dear God, thank you for...

Please help me to get better at...

I wish that...

God bless...

Amen!

Draw a picture in each frame to create your own prayer.

Celebrate!

John 2:1-12

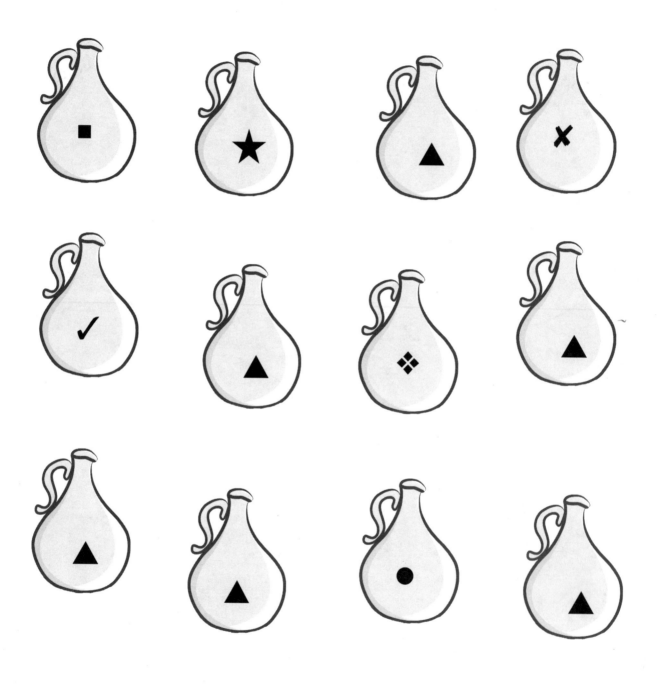

Jesus changed six jugs of water into wine. Circle the six water jugs that are the same.